Suzanne Ruthven was born in 1952 in Northampton and has spent many years investigating the occult. Those investigations have resulted in the publishing of
Malleus Satani - The Hammer of Satan,
a frank, and at times, startling examination of modern Witchcraft and Satanism. By discarding standard textbook references and viewing the Craft from 'inside the circle', Ruthven has produced the definitive work for all those fascinated by the occult.

Shortly to be published, her two novels
Whittlewood and *The Ligeian Testament,*
have been based on current research and attempt to transpose genuine occult lore into highly readable fiction in the modern Gothic horror genre.

**Dedicated to Chris Bray
with gratitude,
admiration and respect.**

"Learn about a pine tree from a pine tree, and about a bamboo plant from a bamboo."
                Basho

"I shall teach you nothing that you do not know. I shall merely lay aside the wrappings of prejudice and bad logic, and show you the real image which you possess in your soul."
                Arthur Machen

"Evil is simply misplaced force. It can be misplaced in time: like the violence that is acceptable in war, is unacceptable in peace. It can be misplaced in space; like a burning coal on the rug rather than the fireplace. Or it can be misplaced in proportion; like an excess of love can make us overly sentimental, or a lack of love can make us cruel and destructive. It is in things such as these that evil lies, not in a personal Devil who acts as an Adversary."
                Qabalah

"He who affirms the devil, creates or makes the devil."
                Eliphas Levi

MALLEUS SATANI : The Hammer of Satan
Suzanne Ruthven

ignotus

ignotus press
BCM-Writer, London WC1N 3XX

Copyright (c) 1994 Suzanne Ruthven

All rights reserved. No part of this publication may be reproduced, stored in a retrieval system, or transmitted, in any form or by any means, electronic, mechanical, photocopying, recording or otherwise, without the prior permission of the publishers and copyright holders.

British Library Cataloguing in Publication Data
(to be applied for)
ISBN: 0 9522689 0 6

Library of Congress in Publication Data
(to be applied for)

Cover design: Susan Preston.

Printed in Great Britain by
Antony Rowe Ltd. Chippenham

Contents

Chapter 1 - Hail Satan! - page 7

Chapter 2 - The Occult Census - page 20

Chapter 3 - The Satanic Myth - page 33

Chapter 4 - History & Heritage - page 47

Chapter 5 - The Devil To Pay - page 63

Chapter 6 - Sex & The Devil - page 78

Chapter 7 - Witchcraft & Magic - page 95

Chapter 8 - From Inside The Circle - page 109

Chapter 9 - The Seige of the Sorcerer's Apprentice - page 124

Chapter 10 - Media Assassination - page 138

Chapter 11 - An Unholy War - page 152

Chapter 12 - The Counter Offensive - page 164

Conclusion - page 178

Appendix I-IV page 179

Bibliography & Sources - page 187

Index - page 190

AUTHOR'S NOTE

Despite hundreds of years of suppression and persecution, it is an inescapable fact that the occult practices of Witchcraft and Satanism have survived (admittedly with some embellishments), in the hearts of a few and the minds of many. With a growing public interest in occultism, this book sets out to investigate the facts behind the practice of modern Witchcraft and Satanism. Also to expose the often fraudulent, bogus and unreliable sources that are offered by so-called experts on the occult, who frequent the media centre stage.

There will, of course, be accusations that the *Malleus Satani* is, by qualification, anti-Christian because the author has consorted with Occultists, Witches and Satanists in order to research the subject as objectively as possible. However, it should be pointed out that my own personal philosophy is centred in Zen-Buddhism-Shinto but this does not prevent recognition of occultism *per se*, as a reflection of many genuine belief systems on the mystery Path, and although not a true adherent, I am a 'soul-friend'.

So why the decision by a non-practising occultist to attempt a non-fiction book on the subject of the occult? It is a question for which there is no logical answer but I have learned from past experience never to ignore such inexplicable impulses; a feeling endorsed by the late Dion Fortune in her book on *Psychic Self-Defence* in which she relates a similar experience of outside stimuli concerning one of her own works. I would like to echo her sentiments:

"... The task is not of my seeking, but as it has come into my hands, I will do my best to discharge it honourably ..."

IGNOTUM PER IGNOTIUS
(To reach the unknown through the still more unknown.)

London 1994

Chapter One   Hail Satan!

SATANISM! A word that stimulates the imagination far beyond the dictionary definition of 'a diabolical disposition, doctrine or conduct; the deliberate pursuit of wickedness; Satan-worship'. Combine this with Witchcraft, Black Magic and the Occult and you have a sulphuric pot-pourri guaranteed to produce shivers of fear, shrouded by macabre fascination, in all but the most blasé of individuals.

But what exactly is Satanism?
In the occult anthology, *The Necromancers*, Peter Hailing included a previously unpublished report that Rollo Ahmed wrote shortly before his death. In this he claimed that black magic was the cause of damaging moral and mental effects amongst intellectual men and women who became embroiled in left-hand path covens. Ahmed, author of the 'widely quoted reference book', *The Black Arts* and occult advisor to the celebrated novelist Dennis Wheatley, claimed strong occult powers for himself, and even admitted to attending a great number of satanic rites during his investigations into black magic.

His report stated categorically that blood sacrifices of animals took place and that human sacrifices were not unknown; even suggesting that some 'missing persons' may have fallen prey to cults which went to those extremes. Such cults, Ahmed alleged, offered sexual indulgences both natural and perverted, in fact, unbridled indulgence of "the senses without censure - money, revenge, material and psychic power."

According to Ahmed, these cults were almost impossible to enter due to their sailing close to the confines of the law in the taking of drugs, sadistic rites, flagellation and intense cruelty in carrying out sacrifices. He even cited older members of the group as being "intellectual people with fascinating ways" who enticed the young and, having gradually overcome their initial scruples, introduced them to drugs and sexual abandonment. "The cult takes delight in blackmail, and destroying marriages, reducing women to alcoholism, drug addiction and prostitution."

However, even this expert testimony, frequently used to support the reality of the existence of modern devil worship, does not pass muster when scrutinised through the eyes of genuine occult practitioners. A leading British occultist considers that Ahmed's comments and opinions are highly suspect, and in many instances provably inaccurate, so how much of his writing really was based on first hand experiences is impossible to gauge. For no matter how competent the occult historian, it is doubtful whether such black groups cited in his writings would encourage the presence of an outsider, especially one who made a living with his pen! It has been suggested that people like Ahmed belong to the world of occult literature that existed before REAL occultists began to write books for genuinely interested seekers.

Nevertheless, Rollo Ahmed's observations do reflect the image that most people carry in their minds of a charismatic leader ensnaring the young and wealthy by promises of spiritual adventure and some form ritual sacrifice. Hundreds of cults have sprung up in America and the UK during the last twenty years; cults which usually target the 18-24 age group, subjecting them to intensive indoctrination in self- sufficient, isolated locations where the outcome is a fanatical following of absolute and unquestioning loyalty to their leader. There have been two well-documented cases in recent years where large numbers of men, women and children have been persuaded to turn their backs on home and family to follow a manipulative religion, only to meet with death at the hands of their founder.

The most infamous examples involve the characteristic catalogue of under-age sex, physical abuse, mind games, and possible murder. Namely the mass suicide in Guyana of members of the American based People's Temple under the guidance of Jim Jones where 912 men, women and children perished by drinking *Kool-Aid* laced with cyanide in 1978; and the recent 1993 Waco debacle in the USA where some 80 members of the Branch Davidians under the control of David Koresh were incinerated after a 51 day siege. Dark, diabolical doctrine, yes - but most are based on ***biblical writ*** not any form of satanic teaching.

Conversely, there has never been a genuine legal investigation or trial that has proved conclusively that occultism has been responsible for any instance of organised or ritualised crime. What we have seen is a growth of journalistic 'buzz-words' and hundreds of books purporting to tell the truth behind the blasphemous rites of coven practice that have distorted the picture beyond recognition. In order to unravel the public misconception of occultism, it would be necessary to scrape away all the fictional trappings and examine events from inside the circle. Satanic conspiracy theories have been with us for hundreds of years and it is almost impossible to detect where fact ends and fantasy begins, for they are indelibly implanted in the public subconscious. However, one fact is inescapable - ***that Satanism only exists where Christianity exists.***

Traditionally, Satanism and/or devil worship can be identified from numerous classical texts as being a darkened mirror-image of Christianity, insofar as all Christian principles, symbolism and ritual are reversed. The inverted cross which presided over the black mass, was reviled by Witches attending the sabbat and who paid homage to the Devil by kissing him under the tail. Their drunken revels included a whole range of sexual perversions; the sacrifice of unbaptized babies, obscene acts involving a stolen host and the more mundane recital of the Lord's Prayer backwards.

In more modern times, journalists have identified vast underground satanic conspiracies that threaten the entire social structure of the western world. According to the reports, thousands of missing children and teenagers in America and Britain are regularly sacrificed to the Devil by an impressive network of satanic witches and warlocks. Dubbed 'satanic survivors' by the press, many who claim to have taken part in the rituals have subsequently turned to Christ and written books to warn others about the dangers of venturing into the dangerous under-currents of occultism in any form. Hundreds of other 'survivors' are currently undergoing therapy to help them deal with the traumas of alleged ritual abuse, in many cases, by members of their own family.

From the medieval historian's point of view, however, the first Papal allegations of devil-worship were levelled at the wide range of non-Christian religions that evolved during the Middle Ages. The reason for this was, according to Professor Jeffrey Richards in his examination of minority groups of the period, the result of a great spiritual revival in the late 11th century, when the Church was 'rescued from decadence ... by a succession of vigorous reforming popes'.

During the next three centuries, under Papal license, the Church systematically cleansed its own Augean Stable of the Templars, Cathars, Waldensians, Bogomils and Jews under the charge of heresy. But since the Church has always identified the world-wide range of non-Christian religions as 'satanic' (including the activities of some of its own reforming clergy, the charges give no clear, objective representation of the alternative religious beliefs of the time.

On the other hand, the Church, in its mass extermination of those identified as heretics and others who refused to acknowledge its confining doctrinal rigidity, created a 'synthetic image' of what it supposed to be the typical Satanist. Professor Richards' brilliant book, *Sex, Dissidence & Damnation* cites a 12th century document by one Walter Map, archdeacon of Oxford which gives the first mention of the obscene kiss and unbridled sex as heretic practice; by the 14th century the connection between the Devil, heretics and lecherous behaviour became a standard accusation.

However, it was not until the mid 14th century, that Witchcraft came into the picture. Professor Rossell Hope Robbins in *The Encyclopedia of Witchcraft and Demonology* states that prior to this period, Witchcraft only carried the death penalty if 'some concrete injury resulted' - other aspects, such as divination and healing, were viewed in the same jaundiced light as prostitution and dealt with accordingly.

Legislation was stepped up to target sorcery and magic, and around this time traditional Witchcraft began to metamorphose into an identifiable practice of satanic involvement which has permeated through to modern times. According to Hope Robbins, Witchcraft was introduced and spread by the Inquisition who assumed control over the delineation of Craft practices, resulting in works such as the *Malleus Malificarum - The Hammer of Witches* (1486). This was the first manual to codify the heresy of Witchcraft and include the now familiar terms such as 'pact' and 'possession'; and a "belief that there are such things as Witches is so essential a part of the Catholic faith that obstinately to maintain the opposite opinion savours of heresy."

Generally speaking, although academics usually have little or no experience of initiated Witchcraft, some do manage to present a valid and objective case for defining the practice from the historian's point of view.

Such was the case with Jeffrey Richards, whose academic study of minority groups in the Middle Ages illustrates how the Church attempted to either control, or in some cases, eliminate them. Richards is Professor of Cultural History at the University of Lancaster and cites Norman Cohn's research, demonstrating how the Church managed to create a "new and wholly artificial construct out of four previously separate and distinct elements: folklore, Witchcraft, ritual magic and Devil- worship."

This new formula effectively concealed the true distinction between high and low magic, ie. that used for good or evil ends. Professor Cohn opined that medieval Witchcraft was essentially low magic focusing on the traditional medicine of the local wise woman who was skilled in herbal healing and midwifery. This was largely confined to the lower classes in the community and practised by individuals rather than groups.

High magic was considered to be a science, practised by learned men involving formal rituals, books of magic lore (grimoires) and the conjuring up of spirits. The most important point was that the Magi *invoked God and not the Devil,* and that the demons summoned were servants to do the magician's bidding, not as masters instructing the Magi in the Devil's work. "Neither form of magic involved the worship of the Devil, orgies, infanticide, or cannibalism." he concluded.

Despite this fabrication of satanic influences, however, one Ludovicus estimated that at least 30,000 men and women were burned between 1450 and 1598 on charges of Witchcraft; by 1550 Witchcraft was formally identified as "an elaborate theological notion" and even became enshrined in civil Protestant regulations despite the schism with Rome.

The conflagration started by the Inquisition continued into the 18th century, by which time an estimated 13 MILLION people had died as a result of their machinations.

... In the deep, dank recesses of the imagination there is always the vision of a vaulted subterranean chamber. The impenetrable stone walls suppurating moisture like globules of blood, glisten in the candle-light, as flickering cowled shadows perform a sinister dance macabre by the high altar. The fetid air mingles with the reek of incense as the high priest prepares to conduct the most blasphemous of all satanic rites of the Witches sabbat - the Black Mass ... (Udolpho. Journal of The Gothic Society)

Although such fictional portrayal of satanic 'covens' are due to the creative imagery of the literati, there have been groups of people, notably the aristocracy and clergy of the 17th and 18th centuries, who formulated satanic underground movements for the gratification of the flesh, rather than any real interest in genuine devil worship or magical practice. The most famous, of course, being the Hell-Fire Club at Medmenham Abbey in Buckinghamshire and it was probably on similar 'private' entertainments in Paris that J. K. Huysman based his satanic novel, *La Bas ('Down There')*.

The similarly misleading 'Satanic School' was the ill-chosen name bestowed by Robert Southey on Lord Byron and his imitators, and applied to other writers charged with deliberate impiety and a total disregard for social proprieties of the day. Since the membership included some of the greatest English writers - Byron, Shelley, Moore and Bulwer - and a number of French ones - Rousseau, Victor Hugo, Paul de Kock and George Sand - it suggests an element of literary vitriol, since Southey's own youthful activities cannot be said to have been exemplary. However, it does serve to illustrate how glibly the term 'satanic' has been used to describe anything that might be construed as immoral or anti-social, even in an age where immorality amongst the intelligensia appeared to be the norm rather than the exception.

From Milton, Dante and Marlowe through to modern film versions of *The Omen* and *The Exorcist*, Satan has presided over literary fabrication to such a degree that the journalistic use of those well worn 'buzz-words' became geared towards boosting the circulation of tabloid newspapers rather than any desire to acquaint the public with factual background information concerning the occult. Adding fuel to the satanic myth, the published confessions contained in the biographies of the satanic survivors produced a horrific blue-print of sexual degradation and ritual abuse that characterised the alleged activities of Witchcraft and Satanism for the next two decades, despite the authors showing a remarkable ignorance of occult practice - even those purporting to have been members of satanic covens for many years.

By the late 1980's satanic hysteria swept through America as a result of the McMartin Pre-School Trial, when the Principal of the school was alleged to have sexually abused hundreds of children in his care. The trial lasted five years and ended in January 1990 - having cost the US taxpayer $30,000,000 - with the acquittal of the defendants, but the seeds of 'satanic child-abuse' had already been sown. The trial had also acted as an efficient propagator of fundamentalist jingoism as the media experimented with banner headlines, such as 'Top-Level Probe into Satan Row', 'Satanic Ring Forces Families To Suffer From A Hell On Earth' and 'Woman Made To Watch Human Sacrifice'.

Satanic hysteria crossed the Atlantic in the spring of 1988, when a news item on Radio Aire reported an astonishing attack in the House of Commons against Witchcraft and occultism in the UK, which was guaranteed to attract extensive media coverage. By citing several trials which would prove conclusively that Witchcraft and child abuse went hand in hand, journalistic zeal for sensationalism resulted in the following accusations being levelled at practising Witches through an eager media network.

(i) That Witches are in league with the Devil and actively work against Christianity.
(ii) Witches by qualification sexually molest children in their rites.
(iii) Witches undertake ritual sex in order to secretly produce babies which are then sacrificed to the Devil.
(iv) Witches implicate feeble willed people into their practices and then sacrifice them or, if the candidate withdraws, blackmail them
and drive them to suicide.
(v) Witches form a conspiratorial sub-society within Britain at all levels of political power and such crimes as are alleged are committed more and more frequently as Witches gain power.
(vi) Some Witches call themselves white Witches and dabble in magic for what they consider good purposes but they are simply misled

because the real power lies with black Witches or Satanists who form the majority.
(vii) In consequence all Witchcraft must be made illegal and the Witchcraft Act re-instated.

Understandably the allegations gained a great deal of coverage in the press (both intellectual and tabloid) and much television and radio exposure; although as far as the general public were concerned, at its inception this particular facet of the anti-occult campaign attracted little real attention. From the safety of Parliamentary privilege, one of the country's leading occult suppliers was named as being "a flashmail order centre for those engaged in occult practices", thereby implying that its proprietor encouraged the atrocities that were allegedly linked to Witchcraft.

The allegations sparked off the usual rash of sensational articles in the tabloids and local newspapers but it was the startling revelations that began appearing in respected national 'glossies' and serious newspapers that caused more than a stir when they hit the high street newsagents during autumn of the same year.

These feature articles pulled no punches in informing their broad-minded, outward-thinking middle-class readership that "in contemporary Britain, Satan is alive and well." According to the in-depth feature articles, the UK was in the "grip of a sinister and murderous trend of child abuse and human sacrifice" which was taking place in British covens; Witches were desecrating churches, and in worshipping Satan, would practice any abomination in his name. Authors unquestioningly accepted that those willing to offer information and be interviewed, had irrefutable proof of their allegations, and several individuals whose names would become synonymous with the campaign to discredit occultism in the UK began to appear regularly in the media.

Public interest was finally ignited following sensational television reporting in the summer and autumn of 1989. The programmes involved had established a formidable reputation for themselves in confronting frauds and con-men who preyed on hapless members of the community and were considered the champions of the unsuspecting who had fallen victim to the unscrupulous. By tackling an emotive subject such as 'satanic child-abuse' the public were indeed now willing to believe that such a horror existed.

From that time onwards, satanic hysteria, fueled by sensational tabloid reporting, was never out of the media spotlight. Several of those claiming to be in possession of factual evidence of satanic criminality, made an increasing number of radio and television appearances to warn parents against the dangers of children dabbling with the occult. For five years the public were assailed with the unspeakable horror of child murder and mayhem, the details of which had been supposedly compiled into a secret dossier, ready to be handed to the Home Office for investigation.

So what happened to that dossier? Where was the evidence? Why were the witnesses never produced? Why, after four years of intense media hype, did the anti-occult campaign evaporate into thin air?

The answer was simple. From the very beginning the one thing that was apparent to anyone with any *real knowledge* of occultism, was the lack of factual, inside information concerning the practice of Witchcraft and Satanism. It was obvious that the experts so freely quoted by the media knew as much about the subject as Genghis Khan knew about community work, and the majority of those publicity seeking individuals who gave interviews about their Pagan beliefs did nothing to convince the public that the world of occultism was not populated by lunatics.

It could possibly be argued that journalists and programme researchers did not know where to lay hands on a bona fide occult expert for advice, but even that excuse would not hold up under examination. In April 1989 The Sorcerer's Apprentice Press had published *The Occult Census* which was distributed to all the editors of national newspapers, television companies and anyone else who had been involved in the publishing or broadcasting of anti-occult material.

Although two promulgators of satanic hysteria had written books about Witchcraft, it was highly questionable whether either of these nationally acknowledged 'leading authorities' on occult matters had ever set foot in a coven, or interviewed a genuine Satanist, and therefore any claim to be fully conversant with the climate of modern occultism was an extremely dubious one. The fact that none of these experts (including those who claimed to be satanic survivors), demonstrated any definite knowledge concerning the tenets and lore governing the occult, was abundantly clear by the repeatedly misleading and false information given in statements to the press.

If the 'leading authorities' were unable to differentiate between black and white magic, Witchcraft and Satanism, they were certainly unqualified to advise the public. Nevertheless the media swallowed every story that was offered without bothering to check whether the information they were being given had any degree of authenticity. That the facts were circulated by accredited members of the Establishment obviously made them exempt from doubt. Nothing appears to have been verified, and even *The Sunday Times* managed to get the pentagram upside down in its touching cartoon of doomed children following a satanic piper.

So where were the genuine occult experts? Why weren't they invited to take part in the interviews and documentaries? Were they afraid to expose themselves and their activities to public scrutiny? Were there really murderous satanic cults operating across America and the UK as suggested by many best-selling authors? Was the practice of Witchcraft really such an abomination? Just who were the Satanists?

There was only one way to separate fact from fantasy, and fantasy from fabrication - and it would not be discovered in the tried and, by now, exhausted sources of reference repeated with depressing regularity over the years. The answer was to make contact with experienced occultists, Satanists and Witches; some of whom had been directly affected by the repercussions of satanic hysteria. And if, as the anti-occult campaigners maintained, both were morally depraved and dangerous, then it would be an investigation doomed to failure.

Nothing could have been further from the truth. There was little difficulty in reaching mature, responsible and intelligent people who were able to discuss their occult involvement honestly and openly. And from the very beginning of the anti-occult campaign in 1988 until the *Malleus Satani* was completed in 1994, the author journeyed through the complex, fascinating, and often surprising realms of Magic, Witchcraft and Satanism which bore little resemblance to the world of historian, fundamentalist, journalist or satanic-survivor-turned-author.

What was apparent, however, even in the early stages of the investigation was the depth of ill-will between the various occult factions. Many Witches were openly hostile to Satanists, consigning them to a spiritual kindergarten, while Satanists were openly contemptuous of the Wiccans and Pagans. Even the Witch-cult was divided against itself, with differing factions constantly sniping at each other through the pages of Pagan journals and this presented a problem in finding an objective starting point.

There seemed to exist an overall blanket of disagreement surrounding Craft policy and procedure, peppered with a large portion of elitist smuggery which forced one Pagan to observe: "Traditionalists still look down their noses at Gardnerians, who cannot always bring themselves to see eye to eye with Alexandrians. Everyone sneers at the Seax-Wicca; Hereditaries want nothing to do with anyone. Those 'in' the Craft treat the uninitiated neo-Pagans as outsiders and consequently (and understandably) are regarded with considerable suspicion in return. New Agers are treated as nothing more than a laughable hangover from the late 1960s and some of the exponents of 'High Magic' see themselves as being way above any of us."

The case was stated just as strongly against Satanism; suggesting that anyone who advocated close links between Satanism and the Pagan movement, or that Satanists and Pagans unite in order to combat the repeated attacks by fundamentalists were "either totally misguided or have motives which need serious questioning."

Chris Bray, proprietor of The Sorcerer's Apprentice, the business attacked in the House of Commons outburst, had been given an opportunity on a local radio station to refute the claims by pointing out that Witchcraft was a *bona fide* religion which pre-dated Christianity by hundreds of years and was not in any way connected with devil worship. However, this news item, broadcast three times during the day on Radio Aire (a commercial radio station in Leeds), was neutralised by a child-welfare spokesman, who stated that they had a growing file of atrocities linked to Witchcraft.

Undoubtedly Chris Bray's response was a good scoop for Radio Aire but it was too early in the anti-occult campaign, and too regionalised for it to have any impact against the mounting suspicion of occultism. Nevertheless it was a good place to start, for The Sorcerer's Apprentice was an established business of more than fifteen years standing and well known to most people with serious occult interests as being the foremost supplier of books on ALL religious subjects in the UK. As it turned out, The Sorcerer's Apprentice was to become an important focal point during the unholy war that was about to commence.

In order to define today's concept of the Craft, Chris Bray explained that the meaning of the word 'Witchcraft' has been twisted and misused by the establishment to such a degree, that many modern Witches spurn the word in order not to be misunderstood and now refer to themselves as neo-Pagans or Pagans. There are certain fundamentals of the Pagan faith which ensure a general cohesive approach but these fall into two aspects - the religious and the magical. Whilst many apparently refuse to work magic at all, a Pagan can best be described as someone who adheres to the Pagan belief but who may, or may not, work magic. Pagans who work magic are better termed Witches, insofar as Pagans who don't work magic tend to irk at being labelled Witches.

When the idea for the *Malleus Satani* was first discussed with Chris, he expressed his concern that it would be difficult to give a broad analysis of modern Witchcraft or Satanism due to the fact that if a hundred different Witches/Satanists were interviewed, the results would show a hundred different ways of approaching their belief. Added to this were the difficulties that existed between the various satanic groups, most of whom were more recent off-shoots of Anton LaVey's satanic organisation in America. He suggested that if Satanism *was* to be put in its proper perspective, it would be advisable to contact a representative of the Church of Satan direct.

There were those who wished to use the *Malleus Satani* solely to endorse their support for the feminist movement, political issues, vegetarianism and anti-war propaganda but since those particular Pagans would not, or could not, discuss the deeper aspects of occultism, it was considered that their viewpoints were not representative of the majority. Those who did agree to help confined their responses to matters relevant to their beliefs, rather than confuse the investigation with outside religious, social or political issues - unless those issues infringed their own freedom of belief.

"Learn about a pine tree from a pine tree, and about a bamboo plant from a bamboo," the Japanese poet Basho tells us ... and that was the basic philosophy behind the research for this book. By maintaining a determination to seek out the fundamental truth about the occult, the author excluded discussions with religious zealots or medieval historians, although both were obviously more than competent when it came to the teachings from their own particular reference sources. The historian can produce hundreds of fascinating Inquisitorial texts and documentary evidence from the Witch-trials having never set foot inside a satanic temple ... the fundamentalist will quote endless theological texts from the Bible but will shrink from accepting the invitation to visit a coven and witness a magical ceremony.

Magic, however, is not merely confined to the practice of Witchcraft. There are other aspects of occult lore which are far removed from satanic temple and Witch coven, and this is what is generally described as the 'High Magic' mentioned above. The ultimate goal of high or ritual magic is not concerned with magical tricks and supernatural effects but the elevation of the magician himself from 'a limited mortal, into what can only be described as a 'superman', fully alive and totally free' *(The Occult Source Book).* It is the harnessing of man's own Will and because it encouraged a wide ranging freedom of thought, the medieval Church immediately outlawed magic and sorcery as heretical practices.

In more modern times ritual magic has been associated with such famous names such as the *Ordo Templis Orientis*, the Hermetic Order of the Golden Dawn, Dion Fortune, Aleister Crowley and others. But despite fundamentalist claims to the contrary, none of these organisations or personalities can be linked to satanic practices. According to *Techniques of High Magic,* ritual magic is a complicated and esoteric doctrine that works on the assumption that the Universe is not a 'mixture of chance factors and influences but an ordered system of correspondences', and that the understanding of this system enables the magician to use them for his own positive or negative purposes.

So ... having established that Satanism and Witchcraft were not synonymous with each other and that there were so many different facets of the occult to be taken into account, it was important to trace the course of their independent histories and understand how *three separate* theologies-philosophies had become so inextricably linked in the public mind that modern thinking was unable to differentiate between them.

Chapter 2: The Occult Census

Before delving into the complicated realm of magic, it was important to segregate and define the occult activities most commonly practised in the UK. By approaching occultists who had already 'come out' in an attempt to stem the tide of anti-occult hysteria at source, it was possible to pinpoint, with some accuracy, the pattern of misleading statements made in the media concerning the nefarious practices of Witches and Satanists

After The Sorcerer's Apprentice had produced its incontestable *Occult Census,* there was no excuse for anyone to ignore the conflicting documentary evidence of a legal and carefully administered census which refuted all of the anti-occult allegations. There was certainly no evidence that had been presented in a court of law that proved Witchcraft and Satanism were inextricably linked to ritual child abuse, nor that Witches actively worked against Christianity. The only claims supporting the allegations of women being made pregnant so that babies could be used for sacrifice, existed only in the books and statements of satanic survivors.

The development of the Christian Devil was in no way connected to Witchcraft and the erroneous usage of the terms 'black and white magic' only served to demonstrate the total lack of basic knowledge in those claiming expert status. It had also been claimed that Witches implicate feeble willed people into their practices but the results of *The Occult Census* indicated quite the opposite.

Shortly before he died in 1954, Gerald Gardner wrote: "I think we must say goodbye to the Witch. The cult is doomed, I am afraid, partly because of modern conditions, housing shortage, the smallness of modern families, and chiefly by education."

Ten years, later a survey in *New Society* by Joan Westcott estimated that there were 400 practising Witches in Britain and observed that by the 1960s Witchcraft was no longer considered to be the province of semi-literate country folk but had permeated the professional and middle classes.

In 1969, Alex Sanders told an interviewer that there were some four thousand, with the numbers increasing steadily; also confirming that it was not the hippies of the day who were being initiated into the Craft, but representatives of the middle class, professional group.

Gardner would probably have been delighted with the results of *The Occult Census* carried out in 1989 which, when viewed in its proper perspective, will probably prove to be the most influential publication on the occult since the *Malleus Maleficarum*. The Census estimates that there are now over 250,000 occultists (including some 150,000 Witches/Pagans), throughout the UK, in addition to the hundreds of thousands of people with a serious interest in astrology, alternative healing techniques and psychic powers.

But perhaps the most important information revealed by The Census is that contrary to popular opinion, occultists are of above average intelligence and pursue a cross-section of professional and middle-management occupations. The following is a brief extract from this illuminating document which should dispel many of the claims perpetuated by anti-occult reporting concerning the dangers associated with occultism in the public mind.

Chris Bray, proprietor of The Sorcerer's Apprentice, is an experienced occultist, lecturing and consulting on all aspects of occultism and knowledgeable up to an adept level in most. Having undertaken the daunting task of master-minding The Census, he was quick to point out that although there may be people who know more about occultism than himself ... "it certainly won't be members of the clergy and their coterie of self-confessed, self-styled Witch-queens who trundle out their obnoxious tales about supposed prior involvement in devil worship and the harm it did them before they turned to Jehovah. If you want to know about a subject then ask an expert. This is no arrogance. I and those within my scope are experts on occultism, not pundits, and *The Occult Census* was organised by, and reveals the truth about genuine occultists."

The Occult Census was designed to be a one-off project and so The Sorcerer's Apprentice constructed the census form to gather the widest possible scope of information which would be of value in many different applications over a long period. They were trying to discover the validity of the occultist's views and had to devise a method of allowing the form-fillers to specify their own classifications and scope instead of offering them a few restricted alternatives which would distort the conclusions. On many questions/topics participants were asked for their opinions which were then aggregated into definitive responses.

The Census was therefore unique in that important sections were delineated by occultists themselves by common and autonomous agreement and grew to reveal the true opinions of those who took part. The Census also included much personal information and it is testimony that, despite the possible risks (imagined or no) there were so many occultists who felt strongly enough to answer all the (sometimes impertinent) questions in order to take this opportunity to get the genuine perspective of occultism across.

Distribution of *The Occult Census* was achieved in various ways. The Sorcerer's Apprentice staff mailed out forms in their thousands to publishers of occult-related magazines and these were inserted in subsequent issues along with editorials supporting the scheme. Most British occult shops and bookstores were sent forms in bulk to be distributed amongst their clientele, whilst forms were also sent in large quantities to most magical orders and groups, associations and clubs for circulation amongst their membership. In order to ensure an even and non-distorted response from right across the occult spectrum, care was taken to include virtually ALL occult contacts and magazines in the UK.

Identification was limited to a dated signature and the inclusion of that person's postcode. Postcodes have an algorithm which meant that each form could be corroborated as genuine without a full address being present. Further corroboration occurred when the form was posted, with the Post Office franking the device displaying date and area. As soon as the form was received it was checked for validity and then all the details (except for names) were entered into a computer, using a suite of programmes which had been specifically written for it. It was obvious to Chris Bray that the accuracy of *The Occult Census* would be questioned in some quarters and so the system used was designed to be beyond reproach; they were also quite prepared to have the method and data inspected by referees if necessary.

By using the postcodes, the assessors were able to produce a geographical analysis which showed that the percentage of occultists was fairly constant within the range of the total population and that there were no abnormal groupings of particular interests in any one area of the country. Although they were objective enough to point out that the only distortion was the figure for North-East England which was very much higher than elsewhere.

However, this could simply reveal that as the North-East is the seat of The Sorcerer's Apprentice's operations, the influence and distribution of census forms led to a disproportionate return in that particular area. It could also underline the fact that one of the most active anti-occult campaigners was based in the North-East, and therefore occultists in that area were more aware of the potential danger of the recent propaganda and responded in larger numbers. On the other hand, the organisers knew for certain that there was a great deal of occult activity in the area and the figures may have merely reflected that.

The average age of those submitting census forms was 32 years; with the youngest being 18 and the oldest 81. What may be surprising to non-occultists, is that those taking part in The Census were predominantly male. (62% as against 38% of females), especially as Witchcraft is generally considered by outsiders to be a matriarchal religion. This statistic is supported by the fact that during the research for the *Malleus Satani*, male Pagans were found to be more open and informative about their beliefs than their female counterparts.

Nevertheless it would be a mistake of overlook the feminist attractions of the Craft insofar as Christianity has always victimised its women by accusing them of all manner of diabolical feminine mysteries. In an essay on feminism by Ann Oakley in *Womanwords*, the writer observed that etymologically and historically, four words or roles have been closely related - woman, Witch, midwife and healer. During the transition from the traditional female control of medicine to a predominately male professional discipline in the 14-17th centuries, the social role of the female 'lay-healer' was suppressed, sometimes by extreme methods. Oakley also observes that "the negative appellation 'witch' was fostered by the medieval Church to whom disease was a god-given affliction, and thus a phenomenon which had to be under strict religious control." Paganism places its male and female adherents as equals and gives back to woman her rightful place within the (Pagan) community.

Possibly the most important fact to emerge from *The Occult Census* was the category covering education, careers and occupations, which should dispel the erroneous belief that Pagans come from the ranks of the unemployed, with drug-addled brains and a total lack of moral fibre. Neither are they *passé* flower children left over from the 60s, or eccentric conservationists. 37% of the forms showed some form of College or Further Education; 21% had attended University, while 14% had received some form of Private Education.

80% of the occultists were shown to be 'in vocations considered by most people to be highly respectable and responsible' and in a random selection of 200 occultists there were found ...

1 veterinary surgeon, 4 homoeopaths, 2 doctors, 4 scientists,
4 professional musicians, 3 booksellers, 1 bank clerk, 1 soldier,
2 farmers, 1 linguist, 5 salesmen, 1 psychologist, 2 economists,
3 chefs, 1 book binder, 1 printer, 1 TV technician, 5 typists.
1 driving instructor, 5 typists, 1 jeweller, 4 electricians, 1 pilot,
2 postmen, 1 showbiz personality, 2 social workers, 4 teachers,
1 policeman and 1 politician.

... illustrating that occultists appear to have a higher level of educational ability and socio-economic grouping than the norm - disproving the allegations that occult study or involvement produces self-centred, insensitive, antisocial and base mentalities.

In the category covering general interests, reading and the creative arts came out at the top of the list while sport, normally a popular national interest, came out second to the bottom, only a notch above politics. The number of occultists owing their own cars and homes was higher than the national average, whilst the divorce rate was lower.

Although politics came out bottom as a field of interest, the views on politics and the state of the world, revealed that most occultists showed a keen interest in environmental issues. It appears that occultists have little confidence in the present political system and the nearest party to the ideals of most occultists is The Green Party which embodies the caring and empathic link with Nature and the planet which is at the heart of all occult systems. The Census also showed a widespread concern about ecology, wildlife protection and conservation. To the question "Do you feel strongly about protecting the rights of animals?" - 85% of the sample gave an emphatic: 'Yes!'

Questions relating to experiences of prejudice and discord revealed that the strongest objections came from members of the immediate family the clergy were also fairly high on the list. *The Occult Census* listed other areas of 'mis-understanding' which do nothing to dispel outsiders' ignorance of Craft practices. Top of the list was the media image of devil-worshippers and black magic; while the press in general was blamed for the 'dis-information' concerning occultism. *When asked if occultism could be harmful to society, 65% replied: "When it is abused."*

Those completing Census forms were asked to describe in their own words three fallacies attributed to occultism by non-occultists and by far the greatest percentage (57%) said "It's all devil-worship/Satanism". In second place with 31% came "It's an excuse for sexual perversion", while 29% felt that non-occultists believe both animal and human sacrifice take place.

[In carrying out research for the *Malleus Satani*, the author found that the general attitude of outsiders was one of fascination and curiosity rather than revulsion. Although none of the people questioned seemed to have any clear idea of what belonging to the Craft involved, most expressed a strong interest in learning more about it. While most would read any book available from the library or secondhand book dealer, none would consider going into the local occult shop. Many knew of someone locally whom they believed to be a Witch and were quiet happy to live and let live. Satanism, on the other hand, was considered to be strictly for perverts and to be left well alone.]

Non-occultists need to glean their information from somewhere and those taking part in The Census were asked to define who they considered responsible for misinformation about occultism. The highest portion of blame, which polled some 82% was laid fairly and squarely on the newspapers. 68% of occultists also chose the written-media and magazines but by far the highest percentage of 85% went to the Christian Church, with a further 43% apportioning blame to other orthodox religions. 57% considered that television broadcasts were also guilty of spreading misinformation about occultism. (It should be pointed out that those taking part in the Census were able to tick more than one answer in each category.) A significant 66% placed the late Dennis Wheatley fourth in the league table of those responsible for the misinformed image of the occult today.

Determined to present a fair, overall picture of occultism in the UK, *The Occult Census* encouraged the participation of Satanists, as well as neo-Pagans. The category 'Satanism and the Balance of Good & Evil' examined the application of good and evil magic but only 14% of the sample admitted to having worked evil magic, whilst 73% of the sample worked only good magic. The analysis of occult involvement and interests of those taking part in the Census exploded another myth perpetuated by the media. Only 4% of occultists in the sample confirmed they were Satanists and "the predilection of The Christian Church to pass off all aspects of occultism as Satanism can now be seen for the propaganda exercise it has always been."

The belief of the majority of occultists lies in the field of Paganism and Witchcraft, the subtle differences of which have already been explained. Over 90% of occultists in the sample claimed to have experienced some form of psychic phenomena, indicating that those who are naturally psychic gravitate towards occultism and over three quarters of those taking part believed in reincarnation. Those practising occultism did so because they felt it develops a sense of spirituality, brings balance and harmony, provides them with an alternative way to master life; offers a genuine faith which is less repressive and encourages freedom; bestows strength in difficult times and gives better understanding.

The summary of The Census produced first-hand evidence that genuine occultists are not devil worshipping and are not involved in evil practices; they are not criminals or sex fiends and do not sanction child-abuse or sacrifice animals; their beliefs are not anti-Christian, non-religious or idolatrous. Neither are they illiterate but responsible, thinking members of society who really care what happens to the planet and the people in it. Occultists are independent and self reliant people who attempt to help others and are not part of a conspiracy to undermine society.

Although The Census did not include information on the rituals of Craft practice, it is worth mentioning some of the artifacts used by Witches as part of their regalia, because of the sinister connotations placed on them by media reporting. Nearly everyone has heard of the *Witches' Bible, or Book of Shadows*, but the generally held opinion is that this was the brain-child of Gerald Gardner and subsequently copied by the Alexandrians. According to the Pagan Federation, a Witch may keep a *Book of Shadows*, which contains rituals, discoveries, spells, poetry, herbal lore, and anything of interest to that person. Covens may keep a similar group book, and some traditions have basic information which is passed on to new members by copying from the group's book, but there is no one document taken by all Wiccans as authoritative.

Similarly, the majority of invocations, prayers, charms and spells used by Witches are also of recent innovation, with Mike A. even going so far as to admit that the writing of new rituals is now a 'cottage industry' amongst some neo-Pagans in the USA, which they attempt to pass off as genuine historical material. High Priestess Jan from the West Country is an aspiring writer of Craft poetry and writes many of the prayers and invocations used by her own coven. Cole also admits that but for a few, all the invocations made by himself and Rae are freshly created for that particular ritual, spell or festival. Those frequently quoted in books on the Craft should therefore be considered examples of modern creation, rather than of ancient origin.

For some inexplicable reason, the wearing of cowled robes and masks has played a large part in anti-occult propaganda to such a degree, that in a recent investigation into the Orkney 'satanic child abuse' allegations, the innocuous funeral cloak of a minister was removed for examination, because it bore a similarity to a 'satanic indicator'.

Most Witches wear coloured beads, girdles and jewellery as part of their ceremonial attire; while an article published in *The Cauldron* explained that the wearing of a spirit mask ensures that the wearer achieves an inner harmony with the divine ones, for the mask itself represents the presence of the divinity in an identifiable way. Again these activities are not confined to the Craft, for there is ample demonstration of the wearing of similar ritual clothing in ALL religious rites carried out by different cultures around the world. Robes are usually worn because they are comfortable and, like the dinner jacket, a great social leveller.

Anti-occult propaganda has had much to say on the recruitment of young people. This has been hotly refuted by Paul Greenslade of The Pagan Federation: "We are not a religion that seeks converts in the sense of preaching to the masses: nor do we attempt to subvert others from their own chosen form of worship. Just because Christians and especially the fundamentalists feel this great need to proselytise, they assume others must need to as well."

Paul maintains that anyone who sincerely seeks contact with the Craft will be drawn to the right source. Some Witches now organise discussion groups or hold classes, at which interested parties may form their own opinions about whether the religion is right for them. There are also many good periodicals, Pagan networks or New Age bookshops through which a genuine seeker can make contact with the larger Craft community. "But be warned", he added "despite what you may have read elsewhere, Wicca does not provide a means to gain magical power over others or a cloak for sex-orgies and an amoral way of life. Witches still face considerable ignorant prejudice, while the requirement to 'harm none' is a demanding one. No *bona fide* coven will consider admitting you unless it is absolutely right for Wicca and Wicca is right for you."

Respected Pagan figures such as Michael Howard and Patricia Crowther in fact, discourage those with only a luke-warm interest. Although it has become easier in recent years for people to make contact with Pagan organisations, the newcomer is still faced with numerous obstacles when it comes to finding the right contacts.

Michael Howard recommends that initial meetings should take place in a neutral environment, such as a cafe or pub. Although not the best places for serious conversation, they do provide a safe and relaxed social atmosphere for getting to know people without making any firm commitment. "And" he adds, "if a new contact immediately starts boasting about their magical or psychic powers; how they knew you in a past life; of their 'psychic battles on the astral'; or offer you instant initiation into the secrets of the universe - make your excuses and head for the door!"

Patricia Crowther went on to explain that being accepted as a member of a coven is a slow process covering a period of at least eighteen months since one must get to know the members of a coven, and vice versa. "We have always performed seasonal rites, ie. universal rites, to which the interested party is invited. In this way, they come to know much of what is required of them, if and when initiation takes place. You must also be willing to explain to the neophyte the history of your coven and from whence it came into being. I am speaking from the point of view of the Hereditary Craft."

These views present a different picture to the claims that Witches are only interested in recruiting the young and gullible. Anyone seeking occult contacts for thrills or curiosity, would certainly be unwilling to spend the time required in learning about Craft practices, and would therefore be judged unsuitable for further encouragement. It is a major step for anyone of any religious persuasion to discard familiar beliefs and take up a new faith, and the High Priestess or Priest of the coven would need to make sure that any neophyte recognised the full implications such a change would bring.

The Pagan Federation receives sacks full of correspondence from those with a genuine interest in learning more about the Craft and as a result, now have a team of ten experienced Pagans answering the letters and enquiries. Where possible, they put people in touch with groups in their area, advise on open meetings, give general information on suitable books and magazines, recommend reputable occult shops and deal with "whatever else people are asking about".

Nevertheless, newcomers are also warned about the authenticity of some of the advertisements appearing in some Pagan contact magazines. Miriem Clay-Egerton attacked those who are always advertising for members and claiming that they want 'right-hand path only'. "If what they mean by equating the right-hand path with so-called 'white' Witchcraft, what are they doing assuming titles like 'High Priestess'? By such advertisements they merely advertise the high level of factual ignorance of that particular priestess. How did such people get to be 'High' Priestesses? In effect they are so imbalanced in basic occult knowledge that they don't know their left-hand path from their right."

She explained that since the times of dynastic Egypt, the Left Hand Path has been the feminine, lunar path of the Goddess; the Right Hand Path has been the masculine, solar path of the God. Much later there arrived on the scene the celebrated Madame Blavatsky and unfortunately, while in India, she had come across the *Varma Marg* and the practices of Viparita Karani. Unfortunate, because she was a product of the Western cultural supremacism of the time, she totally misunderstood and the practitioners weren't falling over themselves to explain their religious secrets to the haughty mem-sahib in what appeared to be purely (or impurely in Blavatsky's eyes), devious sexual practices. She equated the *Varma Marg*, the Left Hand Path, with evil at its worst and said so, loudly and clearly, verbally and in print, all over Europe - with the result that to this day the ill-informed think that left-hand path = evil.

"But," she says, "to get back to our advertising Wiccans. The left-hand path is the lunar, feminine path of the Goddess. Who do they venerate if they claim to worship a right-hand path Goddess? A transvestite?"

Since the publication of The Census there has been a great deal of public concern over the number of occult shops and New Age events springing up in the towns and cities, and much of this anxiety is shared by an increasing number of occultists. New Age interests are attracting more and more people in the exploration of different values but unless those newcomers are lucky, it is easy for them to fall prey to commercial concerns which are operated solely on a business footing. Articles in *The Cauldron* have reflected this viewpoint and expressed concern over the 'consumer' Craft and the fact that instant Wicca is being peddled at weekend courses and workshops, run by those "with little to offer but a desire for self aggrandisement and an insatiable appetite for obeisant acolytes"; together with initiation by post - *for a fee!*

Cole too echoes those feeling in his own inimitable way ... "there is something about the New Age movement that makes me shiver. The way it absorbs all religions, all paths - shake hands with one aspect of it and seven other hands reach out to hold you, lovingly, with compassion, with understanding but no sincerity - and relieve you of your money."

That is not to say that he feels unhappy about the public seeking to know more about the Craft and attempting to understand the practice and observance of the Old Religion. It is the trivialisation of the belief that concerns him...

"Why do I feel uncomfortable when I visit shops that supply occult information? I never used to when it was a seedy, run-down back street place with a few scales, a bong or two, a pile of second-hand books, spider's webs, tarot packs and unwashed, half-finished mugs of tea. Now it's loads of incense, wall to wall carpets, spiritual musak, sliced and diced stones with back lighting. People stand around looking serene and wonderful with all the right jewellery. So why don't I think: Wow, how wonderful, people getting to understand my religion? But I don't."

"There is a new kind of Witch being brought into being. It isn't persistent study, effort, tears and success over the years that gives them birth. It is having a banker's card and the cash to back it up. A sort of Mammon version of what the passage of years and the organic growth of experience brings about in the 'old Witch'. No longer can one trust the old signs of a discreet pentacle, or similar piece of jewellery to recognise another person on the path. Now it's meaningless. Whereas once it was a tricky thing to be a Witch, now people are sure they 'always were one'. They buy the bric a brac and adorn themselves with it, but as for worship of the Horned God and Goddess, forget it. Ask if they have ceased to be Christians and they reach for the Swan Vestas. Something is wrong. It is wrong!"

In addition to a great deal of information concerning the background of U.K Pagans, The Census revealed some surprising attitudes from members of the occult fraternity. The project captured the imagination of many occultists both here and abroad as Chris Bray was quick to recognise; realising that they were taking part in an historic project, many magazine editors were visionary enough to see the possibilities and helped distribute the forms.

However, acceptance amongst some occult underground magazines was more reserved. Most distributed the forms; some included supportive editorials but by then, according to The Census organiser, the "old bugbear of fear of disapproval had set in". The same thing happened with the newly formed S.A.F.F (Sub-Cultural Alternatives Freedom Foundation), and those wishing to remain popular and accepted within their own clique, adhered to the objections raised within their own groups and refused to support it.

Although gratified by the overall response to *The Occult Census* which was considerable, and in the end totally adequate, Chris Bray was disappointed that so many had missed out on the opportunity to give their opinions and views. As many rank and file occultists get their information through privately owned small press magazines, so undoubtedly hundreds of other occultists who would have perhaps jumped at the chance to be part of The Census or join the S.A.F.F, were denied the opportunity by bigotry on the part of a few people who edited the magazines and who were, for whatever reason, antagonistic to *The Occult Census*.

The Census was superbly thought out and a well administered operation, designed to give each and every occultist a formal opportunity of turning the tide of prejudice at no cost to themselves and, in the most anonymous way possible, consistent with a census which would be legally acceptable - and yet still many of those influential occultists who could have made The Census a barnstorming success, refused to back it wholeheartedly. Instead of supporting Chris Bray's efforts to stem the tide of growing the anti-occult campaign, many preferred to ignore it.

This chapter contains only a brief extract from *The 1989 Occult Census* but it does convey an accurate and informative view of occultism in Britian today. Thousands of copies were distributed to all government departments and local authorities; it was included in the National Bibliography by the Copyright Library. Unfortunately, the majority of media representatives failed to investigate further the claims of the Sorcerer's Apprentice's findings, preferring to declare themselves on the side of the 'righteous' rather than the 'right' and ignored the inclusion of what was perhaps the most important piece of information imparted by the Home Office in response to Chris Bray's constant bombardment:

No dossier containing details of child-abuse cases allegedly connected with Witchcraft, or any other evidence that there was a problem of the kind being described repeatedly in the media, had been received at the Home Office.

Chapter 3:   The Satanic Myth

he creation of Satan is the finest example of the goose-quill being mightier than the rapier: but if the Devil plays no part in Witch-lore, where does he come from and how did his presence manifest itself to such a degree that many fundamentalist Christians maintain that to deny the existance of such an entity, is to call Christ a liar! In his *Encyclopedia*, Dr Robbins treats demonology as a complement of Witchcraft but although devils and demons are indigenous to most parts of the globe (ancient and modern) they are not connected with the Old Religion of British Witchcraft.

Doreen Valiente partly answers the question in her Introduction to *Witchcraft - A Tradition Renewed*: "By constantly telling us that there is a great power of evil, personified as Satan, which people can invoke and serve for reward, these good Christians are unwittingly creating the very concept that they denounce. To put it in the words used by occultists, they are creating upon the astral plane a huge thought-form. But this monstrousity is nothing but a mock-up, like the frightful 'demons' created in some film studio for a horror movie. It is time that we demolished it and threw the remains onto the rubbish-heap of human thought."

So who created Satan?

In Christian terms, Satan personifies everything that is evil, corrupt and depraved; he tempts mankind with rich rewards in exchange for mans' immortal soul. Dr Robbins maintains that the Devil or Satan was the creation of incompetent clerics, for in translating the Old Testament into Greek, the Egyptian Jews of the third century BC used the word 'diabolos' for the Hebrew 'satan', an angelic entity whose function was to test mens fidelity to God. He was not originally evil but later became so by 'mis-identification'. When the Greek Septuagint Old Testament was translated into Latin, 'diabolos' became either 'diabolus' (in the early translation) or Satan, in the standard Vulgate text (except in Psalm cix). In the New Testament, however, the Greek word 'santanas' was used to mean something totally different: not an adversary against man, but an adversary against God. Satan's expulsion from the heavenly hosts wasn't due to a fall from grace, but rather a slip of the pen.

Man, Myth & Magic also supports the mistranslation theory in giving the name 'satan' as meaning 'adversary' and not necessarily a supernatural one. The Philistines (1 Samuel, Chapter xxviv) were fearful that David might become their 'satan'. In later biblical passages, a member of the heavenly court appears called 'the satan', whose job is was to act as prosecutor during the judgement of man (Zachariah Chapter iii). After 700BC, when the Book of Job was written, 'the satan' was still acting as a heavenly accuser but was rapidly becoming the bad guy of the scriptures - and from there it was downhill all the way.

It is even possible to detect the origins of evil personified as a goat from the scriptures. The goat first makes its appearance in Leviticus (Chapter xvi) when, following the expiatory rites on the Day of Atonement, the creature was banished into the wilderness carrying the sins of the children of Israel. The goat escapes but laden with the burden of sin - hence 'scapegoat'. Scholars contend that the original Hebrew had no word for 'scapegoat', referring to the sin carrier as 'Azazel'. Since no one knew who or what Azazel was, the translator William Tyndale juggled with the syntax to make sense of the word and came up with the more familiar modern term - the goat became the representation of ultimate sin and Azazel was placed in the hierarchy of demons.

This hierarchy was foremost in the minds of later theologians and it needed a vivid imagination to keep apace with them; clerics of the time were kept busy compiling whole social structures of this hellish and motley collection of evil agitators. According to theologian, Alphones de Spina, exactly 133,306,668 fallen angels accompanied Satan on his explusion from heaven, these subsequently becoming identified as demons. Plutarch ascertained their life span as 9,720 years apiece but Hesiod calculated that demons lived for 688,000 years with the creatures multiplying between themselves, with the aid of incubi and succubi.

Devils and demons have existed in the belief of all ancient and primitive civilisations throughout the world since the dawning of man's history, and it would be the sickest home goal ever scored by mankind if the murder of some 13 million people during the Witch persecutions was due to some idiotic mistranslation from the original Hebrew by a bungling clerk! At this point in history, the Old Religion had been going strong long before the 3rd century BC translation and *even the most devout of believers would be hard pressed to worship an entity that had not yet been invented.*

This confusion over the satanic identity however, was small in comparison with the even more far-reaching repercussions of the biblical *Book of Revelation* or *The Apocalypse*. Its inherent danger lies in the fact that many modern fundamentalist cults actually accept its contents without reservation, although the book itself has long been the subject of vigorous controversy with regard to "its authorship, its integrity and its interpretation". So great is the belief in the word of *Revelation* that its staunchest devotees regularly take trips into the mountains to await the end of the world; and when the Creator refuses to oblige, they trek down again to await the next portentous sign.

The Book of Revelation is purported to have been written by St John the Divine (presumed to be the apostle) and has generally been accepted as such since the 2nd century AD - which is how it managed to get itself tacked onto the end of the New Testament. However, even scholars from those early days questioned its authenticity. Whoever the writer was, it is now commonly admitted that older apocalyptic material had been incorporated in the work, scholars even going so far as to define the areas of 'borrowed elements' and seeing it as a Christian revision of an originally Jewish apocalypse.

A widely held theory maintains that *Revelation* was merely a symbolic narrative of the events of the writer's own time, cobbled together with a great deal of loose apocalyptic material' which was not always understood by the writer himself. Written during the persecution of the Christians by Domitian, it conjured up a profound montage of dream and vision; comforting the persecuted of the present, by promising a divine triumph in the future. Penned at a time when Christianity was struggling for existence, the book was intended to breathe a note of encouragement. A sort of revised Judaic "It'll be all right on the night."

Numerous novelists and scriptwriters have drawn ideas from it, including the popular *Omen* series, which drew its plot entirely from quotations from *Revelation,* in order to send a posse of fanatical priests on a *kamikaze* mission to kill off the antichrist. And out of fiction came more fiction. The term 'antichrist' so familiar in popular novels, only occurs in the two Epistles of John, where it is used to mean either a false claimant to the Messiahship or an antagonist to the true Messiah. The antichrist is even given a definite personality. He is a *Jewish* pretender to the Messiahship, appearing as the end of the world draws nigh to rebuild Jerusalem and gain the allegiance of the world by performing great signs and wonders. Needless to say, the true (Christian) Messiah will come to the rescue of the faithful, shattering the forces of the antichrist and destroying the Zionist usurper. A classic example of thinly disguised anti-Semitism concealed by Biblical writ - but considered by many to be the word of God!

Revelation also introduces us to *gematria,* the antagonistic powers of 'The Beast' and the often-quoted 'Number of the Beast = 666'. The interpretation of this passage rests on the Hebrew and Greek usage of the letters of the alphabet and numbers to supplement their writing. The method of using *gematria* converts the letters of a word into their number equivalents, adding them up and then substituting another word which adds to the same total. Therefore, a writer, whilst avoiding direct mention of a specific person or thing for reasons of self-preservation, could indicate the same by the use of numbers which corresponded to the value of the letters composing the name.

There have been many attempts to solve the riddle of the identity of The Beast and the results have included Napoleon, the Pope, Luther, the Kaiser and Hitler. (Macauley went for the House of Commons because it had 658 members, plus three clerks, a sergeant and his deputy, a chaplain, a door-keeper and a librarian, making a total of 666 in all) According to Richard Cavendish in *The Magical Arts,* it is now generally accepted the The Beast referred to the Roman Empire and its seven heads to the seven Emperors. Attempts have been made to identify both Nero and Caligula, although there have been other permutations based on several other less popular characters of Imperial Rome.

The Church went to great lengths to develop the idea of a potent adversary of all that was considered divine - an earthly representation of evil personified, welded together out of plagiarised passages and spurious identities foisted onto the older gods. Pan, with the horns and lower limbs of a goat, and Cernunnos, the great stag-horned god of the Witches, were ideal, ready-made arch-demons and by subjecting earlier Hebrew texts to a Greek treatment of substitution, amendment and addition, the compilation of The Bible gave humanity its greatest fictional character - *Satan!*

There was very little left on the subject of Hell and Damnation for fertile imaginations to work on until Italy's greatest poet, Dante Alighieri's *La Commedia* (or *The Divine Comedy* as it became known some 250 years later) hit the medieval scholars in the early 14th century. This epic work took Dante around twenty years to write and was divided into three parts: *The Inferno, Purgatorio and Paradiso.*

According to Dante's epic, during Holy Week in the year 1300 the poet was allowed to pass through the realms of the other world in the company of Beatrice and Virgil. After encountering three wild beasts, representing Lust, Pride and Avarice, Dante passed through the Gate of Hell into the Ante-Hell, devoted to those contemptible spirits who lived without blame and without praise, crossing the Acheron to enter the first of the nine concentric circles of Hell proper. These circles are apportioned as follows: (1) unbaptised children and virtuous heathen - Limbo; (2) the lustful; (3) the gluttons; (4) the avaricious and prodigal; (5) the wrathful and sullen - Styx; (6) the heretics; (7) those guilty of violence or bestiality; (8) those guilty of fraudulent malice (which included seducers, soothsayers and sorcerers, hypocrites and thieves); (9) those guilty of treacherous malice.

Dante having now reached the bottom of Hell and the centre of the earth, makes his way back up through the bowels of the earth until he sees daylight again at the foot of Mount Purgatory. Ante-Purgatory is devoted to the expiation of negligence in matters spiritual whilst the seven terraces that circle the slopes of the mountain are occupied by spirits atoning for (1) sins of the spirit of love distorted; (2) defective love; (3) sins of the flesh or love excessive. The division of the vices is set out in Purgatory, while a similar explanation of the divisions of Hell can be found in the Inferno. By now Dante had reached Earthly Paradise and was gathered up through the ten Heavens of Paradise.

Mankind needed no further convincing; all the evidence of a satanic manifestation was there in chapter and verse to be interpreted as they saw fit. Witch-hunters of the 16th century also singled out the story of Faust, regaling the uneducated classes with the dire consequences of trafficking with devils and demons. Already familiar with the story in its dramatic form, the populace mistook drama for reality.

The fact that Faust actually existed has been buried under an avalanche of fiction, but in reality such a man (or possibly twin brothers), lived in Germany in the early part of the 16th century and is recorded as being a 'necromancer, astrologer, alchemist, soothsayer and clairvoyant' *(Man, Myth & Magic)*. Very little is known about him (or them) except that it was amongst the likes of Paracelsus and Cornelius Agrippa that he gained his reputation before disappearing into legend in 1540.

However literati may argue over the origins of the Faust legend, what is painfully obvious is that the obscure little magician replenished the clergy's supply of ammunition, and pacts with the Devil appear in hundreds of European witch-trials. Even Dr Robbins devotes some nine pages to the subject in his *Encyclopedia of Witchcraft & Demonology*, explaining that the pact "pin-pointed sorcery as heresy and thereby brought Witchcraft under the jurisdiction of the Inquisition and was considered to be the very essence of Witchcraft". The Faust story proved to be extremely useful example of what happened to those entering into negotiations with the Devil.

The colourful legend of the man who sells his soul to the Devil seems to have first appeared about the sixth century, remaining popular throughout the Middle Ages in many forms until the first literary version of the story, the *Volksbuch* was published in Frankfurt in 1587. Soon afterwards it appeared in England under the title of *The History and Damnable Life and Deserved Death of Dr John Faustus*. Christopher Marlowe used this translation of the story and his play was probably the first dramatised version of the Faust legend, achieving instant recognition both in England and abroad.

The play retained its popularity long after Marlowe's mysterious death in a tavern brawl in 1593, although Faustus was later remodelled into a sort of Don Juan - by the Jesuits who apparently disliked his scepticism - and it was in this form he came into Goethe's hands. The three chief versions of the old legend: the *Volksbuch* a medieval story in Protestant garb, Marlowe's Renaissance rendering and Goethe's modern Faust, are all representative of the original legend. The *Volksbuch* records Faust's history from his birth to his final dismemberment by the Devil in the gruesome but moral tone of religious righteousness.

Marlowe, on the other hand, gave the character a thirst for boundless power, not merely Goethe's quest for knowledge, but 'all the power that is in the world'. Marlowe did not dismiss the existence of magic and this gave his character "a passionate energy, an emotional sensibility which Goethe's more shifting, sceptical and complex Faust lacks." Such dimensional characterisation as this was entirely out of order with dramatic tradition of the time, and by the fourth edition published in 1616, it had acquired a plentiful supply of retributional horror - not only in the account of Faustus's death but in the description of Hell itself. The modern version of Marlowe's play is certainly not the work as it was originally written and, according to experts, it is evident that parts had been heavily censored, although there is no way of discovering just how much of the original work was cut.

John Milton added yet another dimension to the literary Lucifer depicted in *Paradise Lost*, written after the Restoration. This fictitious archfiend was so magnificently proud, so full of courage, eloquence and arrogant defiance, that the loyal angels of heaven pale into insignificance beside the flamboyant anti-hero. It is highly doubtful whether Milton intended Lucifer to overshadow the Almighty, but he obviously realised (like all commercial novelists) that vice sold more books than virtue. Satan is wicked but like his real-life counterparts, the worse the rogue the greater his magnetism. In an illustration by Gustave Dore for *Paradise Lost*, Satan sits brooding on a rock, 'mean, moody and magnificent' with bat wings extended; his handsome face distorted by a scowl and the hard muscular body concealed only by the wispiest of drapery. In short, Satan had been given virility, while the archangels Gabriel, Michael and Raphael remained pathetically neuter by comparison.

Perhaps Milton realised his error in making Satan too great in *Paradise Lost*, for in a later work, *Samson Agonistes*, he is less awesome and has lost much of the size and dignity that both attracted and repelled the reader. Milton obviously had some empathy for his fallen angel, for although in his private life, three times married Milton was a 'champion of chastity and marital constancy', his portraiture of Satan brings to light some less pure fantasies!

The entire Satanic Myth had been formulated on the early Church's insistance that the Devil existed. Whilst the fictionalised accounts from Dante to Dennis Wheatley merely expanded the fantasy world of arch-fiends, blood pacts and the legions of Hell. This esoteric world of the black magician and those willing to barter with their soul's immortality for a lifetime's pleasure has provided numerous occult novelists with valuable material. And although many of the grimoires (from which much of this information was taken), claim ancient origins, most of those available for study are later 16th and 17th century manuscripts, such as the *Lemegeton* or *Lesser Key of Solomon*, which contains impressive instructions for the evocation of some seventy-two demons.

Echoing the more recent findings of Professor Kieckhefer, the late Arthur Waite cited the *Histoire de la Magie en France* (1818) by Jules Garinet who "speculates that the monks, who abused public credulity for the sake of diversion amidst their idleness, may have assumed ridiculous disguises, and may themselves have committed the extravagances which they attributed to devils". The same author affirms, as 'certain and incontestable', that in all the criminal trials of sorcerers and sorceresses the scene of the Sabbath (sic) was invariably in the neighbourhood of a monastery. "Since the destruction of the monastic orders," he concludes triumphantly, "no more is heard of such assemblies, even in places where the fear of the devil still exists. Add to this that seventy-five years later, Papus, the French occultist, would persuade his readers that all the Grimoires of Black Magic were the work of priests ..."

The cult of Gothic fictional horror perpetuated the myth of the Devil interfering with man's existence and became popular reading for the educated classes. But no occult fiction writer could have penned a more perfect exit from this world than the reality surrounding the burial of Matthew Lewis. Dark storm clouds were scudding across the skies of the Atlantic when his coffin, wrapped in a weighted hammock, was consigned to the deep on 14th May 1818. Almost immediately, the coffin bobbed up again and the loose canvass, now acting as a sail, steered it off in the direction of Jamaica until it finally disappeared over the far horizon. The bizarre funeral was a fitting end to Lewis - novelist, poet, playwright and Member of Parliament - who had written the century's most controversial book *The Monk*.

Although not a totally original work, *The Monk* catalogues an impressive collection of supernatural horrors, skilfully arranged into a tale of a debauched monk. Surrounded by cameos of chilling cruelty borrowed from nearly every writer of horror fiction published at that time, the main character, having violated his sister and murdered his mother, signs a pact with the Devil in order to escape the clutches of the Inquisition. The publication of *The Monk* in 1796 sparked off heated controversy with its 'shameless and unwarrantable attacks upon the Scriptures', which aroused religious indignation and literary disputes, although, as a result of its popularity 'Monk' Lewis became a literary celebrity in the salons on London.

Other writers and poets jumped on the Gothic bandwagon to cater for the new public interest in the Devil including J. K. Huysmans, whose classic novel of Satanism caused a sensation when it first appeared in 1891 because of the extraordinarily detailed and vivid descriptions of the black mass. The publisher's blurb on a later reprint claimed: "These descriptions are also authentic, for Huysmans had first-hand knowledge of the satanic practices, Witch cults and the whole of the occult underworld then thriving in Paris."

Although Huymans demonstrates an intelligent awareness in his observations on general occultism, his sources are undeniably old Inquisitorial ones and conspicuous for the lack of factual details of initiated Witchcraft. Whatever Huymans underworld connections might have been, they were most certainly NOT Witches nor likely to be Satanists, since neither include any form of a black mass as part of their ceremonies. One suspects he may have belonged to, or been connected with, a group of Parisian 'occultists' whose interests were the intellectual study of medieval mysticism and alchemy, or perhaps the pursuit of erotic pleasure, rather than the practice of magic.

Probably the most talented and yet the least known of all occult fiction writers is Arthur Machen: whose brilliant narrative, attunement with earth forces, receptiveness to the mysteries of Nature and Celtic blood, enabled him to create stories that reflected a healthy respect for supernatural forces at odds with meddling human curiosity. His first success came with the controversial publishing of *The Great God*

Pan in 1894, followed by a series of spine-chilling but beautifully written tales, mostly set in Gwent amid the haunted woodlands and pathways of the Valleys. Unlike many of his contemporaries, however, he never attempted to describe the awesome Great God.

Machen was no dilettante as later books and an biography demonstrate; his perception of mystical matters, particularly those surrounding the Holy Grail legends, were very highly developed. After the death of his first wife in 1899, Machen joined the Hermetic Order of the Golden Dawn (fellow members were Aleister Crowley, William Butler Yeats, Algernon Blackwood and Dion Fortune) but the mysteries, and probably the politics and prima donna antics of his fellows, bored him. His puckish sense of humour would also have put him at a disadvantage in an Order whose members were not recognised for their ability to laugh at their own expense. It does indicate, however, that he held a positive viewpoint on occultism and was not, in the latter years of financial hardship, tempted to use his insight into the Order to supplement his meagre income. He was one of the first writers of occult mystery to realise that hinting at terror was more effective than explicit description and of Machen, Jerome K. Jerome wrote: "For ability to create an atmosphere of nameless terror I can think of no author living or dead who comes near him."

But if the public needed a flesh and blood villian to enforce the new Victorian morality, it had a perfect specimen in Aleister Crowley, whose activities attracted headlines wherever he appeared. Unfortunately, Crowley's unsavory reputation clouded his true abilities as a magician; the majority of ruined lives credited to his malign influence were people of a self-destructive nature and although Crowley's dominance may have accelerated their progress on the downward slope, most of them needed no encouragement to step onto the ice. Crowley's occult powers have never been considered fraudulent (except by the press and the majority of his biographers!), and if he had managed to concentrate his efforts in harnessing his ego, instead of indulging in shock tactics, he would probably been hailed as a true Magi, instead of being tagged with the charlatan label that has dogged his footsteps.

Violently anti-Christian as a result of his Plymouth Brethren upbringing and referring to himself as The Beast (an appellation bestowed on him by his own mother), Crowley was too much of the ego-maniac to contemplate worshipping any fictional satanic entity. His endeavors to commune with higher levels of enlightenment were concentrated on 'the Most Highest and Most Holy' as is borne out by the observations of C. R Cammell and Israel Regardie.

He enjoyed cultivating a reputation for evil but as Anton LeVey, High Priest of the Church of Satan in the USA observes, he spent most of his time as a 'poseur par excellence and worked overtime to be wicked'. La Vey suggests that Crowley also spent a considerable part of his life with his tongue jammed firmly into his cheek and remarks scathingly that his followers of today manage to read 'esoteric meaning into his every word'. Whatever else he may have been, Crowley paid no homage to Satan, despite his sinister public image of 'The Wickedest Man in the World'.

In *The Occult Census* a surprising 66% of the poll placed Dennis Wheatley in fourth place on the table of the 'Who is responsible for the misinformation concerning Witchcraft?' section. It has often, and rightly, been claimed that the myths surrounding the public image of occultism are fostered by those with a vested business interest in keeping it going, ie. films, fiction, media, etc. Many occultists obviously believe that the late Dennis Wheatley had such an interest; writing many inaccurate books on the subject purely for monetary gain and thus re-inforcing the devil-worshipping image of Witches in the public mind.

This charge is possibly a little unfair considering that Wheatley gathered his information from meetings with Montague Summers, Rollo Ahmed and Aleister Crowley, and therefore should not be accused of deliberate irresponsibility in his writing. In his own author's note in *The Devil Rides Out*, he states that he has "spared no pains to secure accuracy of detail from existing accounts when describing magical rites or formulas for protection against evil, and these have been verified in conversation with certain persons, sought out for that purpose, who are actual practitioners of the Art ..."

Wing Commander Dennis Wheatley was no gullible literary hack and had been an important member of the London Controlling Section during the last war; a secret bureau established by Churchill to plan stratagems to deceive the Germans about Allied operations. Their emblem was a small figurine of the Dancing Faun which 'suggested dark and evil spirits at work in tangled forests'. Privy to some of the grimmest secrets of military intelligence, he would be unlikely to have swallowed any information without some personal verification.

The fact that he consulted Ahmed, Crowley and Summers is a strong indication that he made a definite attempt to corroborate the facts, although one occultist's information stated that Wheatley employed students during the summer vacation to research and extract the contents of grimoires in the British Museum, which he would subsequently 'cocktail' into a fictional and highly inaccurate account for a future novel. Since a friend of Crowley's denies that he had any involvement with devil worship, that it was questionable whether he had any interest in Witchcraft and was a notorious practical-joker; that Summers' works are totally inaccurate and only accepted academically because he had been a priest and in 1928 had published a translation of the *Malleus Malificarum* - the bias of the time supposed that to be 'expert knowledge'; and Ahmed is recognised as "a learned occult historian but his conclusions smack of a total lack of experience of real occultism", then it suggests that it was Wheatley himself who was misled. This apparently is no uncommon, for Chris Bray "... could mention a clutch of occult historians who, although great scholars, are absolutely naive and ignorant as far as initiated magic goes".

There is no doubt that Wheatley popularised occult fiction and was probably indirectly responsible for an upsurge of interest in occultism, despite urging anyone in the strongest of terms not to be drawn into the 'practice of the Secret Art'. He had no first hand practical knowledge of what he describes as the 'dark arts' but states that it is his own "absolute conviction that to do so would bring them into dangers of a very real and concrete nature". In view of the circumstances, perhaps his only real failing was in consulting the wrong experts.

Although there are now organisations such as the S.A.F.F (Sub-Cultural Alternatives Freedom Foundation) and The Pagan Federation who are willing to supply information on all aspects of occultism and Witchcraft to interested parties, there existence has done little to combat the bogus 'survivor' novels that have regularly appeared in print during the last ten years. This type of highly dramatised fiction was at first believed to be factual accounts of a child who had been subjected to every kind of degrading practice by a group of Satanists in the USA. It later transpired that there was no shred of evidence to support the outrageous claims made in the books and it is now generally accepted that the so-called victims were only suffering from childhood fantasies. Nevertheless they became international bestsellers and the repercussions were to take on a far more sinister note in the years to come, both in America and Britain.

Over the next ten years, other gruesome fantasies were twisted into fact - with an ulterior purpose; to fuel fundamentalist claims against occult practices. Another of the alleged 'survivor' autobiographies gives lurid and graphic accounts of satanic involvement, regaling the reader with the pitiful details of life as as a stripper, heroin addict and prostitute to the elevated ranks of Satanic High Priestess. Finally being voted Queen of the Black Witches at an unholy bash supported by a 1000 strong gathering on Dartmoor.

Ten years later, after being 'saved by Jesus', the survivor had turned to novel writing and joined the Christian lecture-tour circus. Those who have attempted to check the details of the story are hampered by the overwhelming lack of dates and other corroborating details but what IS blatantly obvious to any experienced occultist - apart from the surprisingly few actual statements concerning Witchcraft and Satanism - our satanic survivor's knowledge of Witch-lore is sadly lacking for one who was raised to such lofty heights!

The most popular forms of occult fiction read today are those written by authors such as James Herbert and Stephen King, who for the most, steer well clear of the Satanist v Exorcist formula that pre-occupied writers in the 60s and 70s. Although the Devil and his black masses may no longer be commercially viable for the publishing houses, the paperback versions have a remarkably long shelf life.

Many of those published in the 1970s have survived *over twenty years of circulation* in second hand bookshops and investigations by the author have shown that these are the sources from which the public gets its information. Whilst most would not go into a reputable occult bookshop and select an informative volume by an expert, they will always pick up a couple of 60p paperbacks on the subject off the second hand counter, along with the weekly intake of thrillers or romances.

It has to be faced that the general public's attitude to occultism IS twenty years out of date and has subsequently been clouded by the inaccurate, misleading and often fraudulent accounts such as those mentioned earlier in this chapter. Perhaps, as Doreen Valiente observes, it is time to demolish the out-dated and erroneous image of Satan and throw it on the rubbish-heap where it belongs.

Chapter 4: History & Heritage

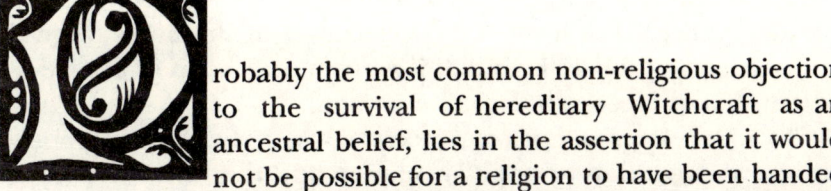

Probably the most common non-religious objection to the survival of hereditary Witchcraft as an ancestral belief, lies in the assertion that it would not be possible for a religion to have been handed down to the present day, purely by word of mouth. As occult author, Michael Howard observed, the Old Religion was certainly fragmented by the years of persecution with only debased remnants surviving under the guise of folklore, seasonal customs and superstition, but does this necessarily exclude the possibility of its survival as an definitive religion?

An important parallel can be drawn between the Old Religion of the British Isles and that of the native North American Indian, whose similar belief system represents examples of 'primal traditions which have existed for some 30,000 years' in the form of a basic Nature religion, with strong shamanistic overtones, ancestor worship, spiritual healing, vision quests, a belief in a highly active spirit world and rebirth. Although the native American Indian was a highly accomplished warrior, he was no match for the white settlers responsible for the genocide of 12 million Indians, through the "introduction of the smallpox, whisky and the bayonet" over a span of 250 years.

The new Americans also intended that centuries of native culture should be obliterated and it was not until the 1970s that the Indians won back their right to worship their own religion and speak their ancestral language, both of which had been officially oppressed for generations. If the native Americans are now returning to their ancestral beliefs which have, through necessity, been handed down verbally and in private for over two hundred years, surely this makes an excellent case for the possibility of the survival of a similar belief elsewhere in the world?

According to W G Gray in *Western Inner Workings*, like the Qabalah, the Old Religion was always handed on from 'mouth to ear', partly because of illiteracy, partly because of an inherited Druidic dislike for writing down what they considered sacred matter, but mainly because of the risk to life if caught by the authorities with such damning evidence in their possession. He also observed that oral tradition *can* be amazingly tenacious, if subjected to local variations, and in this fashion considerable fragments of the Old Religion descended to the present time. Since it saw less persecution in Britain than on the continent, the probability is that it survived in Britain in a somewhat better state of preservation than elsewhere.

To a large degree, our own ancestral history has been suppressed insofar as according to popular opinion and the majority of school text books, the history of the British Isles started when the Romans landed on our shores, engaged in a few isolated skirmishes with the woad-painted locals and started civilisation as we know it. The teaching of history has carefully concealed from generations of school children the inescapable fact that our ancient ancestors were not miserable savages of limited intelligence but a people with a highly developed sense of mystical awareness. Our *recorded* history began thousands of years *prior* to the arrival of the Romans with the Neolithic people - a folk with a penchant for vast circular earthworks, immense earthen barrows for burying their dead, and who laid the first foundations for our greatest archaeological and mystical wonder, Stonehenge.

Around 1800BC, our island saw the emergence of the Beaker people, so named for their early examples of primitive pottery, but better known as the engineers who erected the numerous arrangements of standing stones scattered throughout the land and plotting the intricate courses of the enigmatic ley lines. It is also believed that these were the builders who brought the immense blue stones from the Prescelli Hills in West Wales to the windswept plain at Salisbury. Although very much in dispute, the theory that Stonehenge is "a prehistoric computer, a device for making highly intricate predictions of equinoctial sunrises and sunsets, moonrises and moonsets, and eclipses" *(Man, Myth & Magic)* suggests that our ancestors were considerably more advanced than our present-day teachers would have us believe.

Possibly, the most important and influential invasion of the British Isles was the arrival of the Celts around 1200BC and from whom many of us today trace our descent through Welsh, Irish or Scottish forebears. The predominant religion of the time was that of the Earth Mother and when the Celts arrived on our shores, they discovered a compatible and flourishing form of worship which is generally recognised as being the Old Religion of Witch-lore. Murry Hope in *Practical Celtic Magic,* describes the ancient faith as being a combination of more than one belief; possibly that of the 'Beaker' people, grafted onto an even earlier cult that was indigenous to the native islanders. What is evident is that the Horned God featured prominently in their worship. Not only did the Celts accept the Horned God, they also identified with the worship of the Goddess in her triple form, whom they could associate with their own Epona.

The Celts were also swift to recognise the importance of local ancient holy sites and in particular the Druids, with their vast knowledge of 'cosmogony and inner mysteries', were able to use the holy ground to complement the native beliefs rather than suppress them. If, as it is believed today, the numerous stone circles and monoliths were the key to the ancient energy fields known and mapped out by our primitive ancestors, then the Druids were, according to Hope, 'only too pleased to plug in their power lines'.

It is from these very early times that the symbols of Witchcraft originate. The ancient British Goddess was known as Ceridwen, guardian of the cauldron of life, which was later identified with the Grail of Arthurian legend. There were also nine sisters who guarded the cauldron of rebirth. (*The Elements of the Celtic Tradition* by Caitlin Matthews) "The one who is first among them has greater skill in healing ... she has learned the uses of all plants in curing all ills of the body. She knows, too, the art of changing her shape, of flying through the air ..." This is the earliest appearance of Morgan le Fay, half-sister of Arthur, shown in the guise of healer and shapeshifter.

Those distant days of lofty, mystical enlightenment were soon to plunge into spiritual darkness. The Romans came (54 BC); followed by the Angles, Saxons, Jutes, Danes and the Normans - and with them the spread of Christianity. Despite the heroic efforts of King Arthur and the magical powers of Merlin, native mysticism was replaced by the more commercially minded Anglo-Saxon thirst for money. The Celts retreated to their mountainous strongholds and left the newcomers to trade spiritual integrity for commercial gain.

The ancient civilisation of Britain perished in that 'last dim weird battle of the west' when Arthur fell fighting against the treachery of Mordred. The bards of later ages wove fabulous stories around this last true King of the Britons, and Arthur the warrior became the Arthur of romance - the epitome of Christian chivalry and monarchy. The final insult came when the legend was further Christianized by the introduction of a bogus story surrounding the Holy Grail quest - the Grail itself being an important aspect of the old Witch-cult.

The Old Religion clung on in rural areas and remote regions away from the powerful Christian centres that had sprung up in eastern and southern Britain. In an early study of Witchcraft published in 1952, just one year after the repeal of the Witchcraft Act, Pennethorne Hughes acknowledged that the rituals of primitive magicians may actually have been more effective than anything their modern counterparts could imagine. Hughes suggested that adherents of the Old Religion possessed a form of group-consciousness that enabled them to completely immerse themselves in the collective requirements of the tribe, describing it as as 'psychic sensitivity'; a closeness to and an awareness of, the forces of Nature.

Colin Wilson affirmed Hughes' opinion in *The Occult*, published some twenty years later, that this essential quality had been lost in the earliest stages of civilisation, and that although magic ceremonies through the ages have tried to re-create it, our early ancestors "possessed in their concentrated and united wills, a magic tool that the modern magician envies."

In the early days, Paganism and Christianity existed hand in hand and slowly but surely, Christian churches were erected on the sites of ancient holy places while indigenous traditions and festivals were transposed into the church calendar. There has always been much criticism of Witches hiding themselves away under the cover of darkness and using churchyards for the scene of their activities but it is quite logical, if one stops to consider the fact that in erecting a Christian church on a former holy site, the only time that Craft followers could meet without being disturbed, would be under the cover of darkness in what was now the churchyard. Added to this, as the monthly esbats co-incide with the phases of the moon, it would be perfectly natural for a coven to meet after dark.

To the question of why the great Witch persecutions did not detonate at the beginning of the Church's history, Hughes gives the answer that in the early Middle Ages the influence of the Church was so weak that Pagan beliefs had to be adapted or absorbed into Christian doctrine in order to convert the heathen populace. In the early days it was enough to compromise with a nominal conversion and overlook the rites and beliefs of earlier Paganism, particularly if these events could be superimposed with the name of a recognised saint.

By the end of the 15th century, however, the outlook in mainland Europe was entirely different. There was a new intellectual climate to challenge man's thinking and the drastic measures to stamp out Witchcraft came not from strength but from an establishment facing despair. It was not until the 14th century that the Witch-cult was finally identified by the Church as an immediate threat to the growth of Christianity. Previous punishment had been rather for their injury to man than any offence to God but by the 15th century attitudes had hardened and to the medieval mind, the existence of devil worship was an accepted fact.

Professor Richard Kieckhefe gives an insight into the influence that classical literature had on the viewpoint of the scholastic minds responsible for the persecution manuals. Many fictional works such as Homer and Vigil were cited as historical fact, and the legendary sorceress Circe became a flesh and blood example of personified evil in women. Classical literature, with which the educated of the time would be familiar, contains numerous instances of magical potions and spells used by women to avenge themselves on a jilting lover, an unfaithful husband or a hated rival. Seneca, Theocritus, Lucan, Horace and many others provided the basic Witch-hunt material for the persecutors and in Kieckhefer's own words: "If medieval Europeans had known no other sources for misogyny, they could easily have learned it from these texts."

The Greek goddess Hecate was also introduced into the triple aspect of the Goddess, adding even more confusion in the identification of the original Pagan deity of pre-Celtic times. Sometimes identified with Artemis and having as her emblem the crescent moon amid oak leaves entwined with serpents, Hecate was recognised as

Queen of Ghosts and Witches. In her Artemis/Diana aspect, the Goddess was more benevolent and features strongly throughout Sir James Fraser's, *The Golden Bough* as the Goddess of ancient fertility rites and a more easily identifiable personification of the Goddess of the Old Religion.

It was also at this point that new knowledge was flooding in from Arabia and Robert Graves (in his chapter on Modern Witchcraft included in *The Necromancers*) draws attention to the influences of an imported Saracen cult which was grafted onto local Pagan stock. According to Graves, when the Saracens/Moors invaded Europe and seized Spain in 711AD (soon controlling southern France, Savoy, Piedmont and part of Switzerland), they brought with them their own cult, whose rites consisted of "ecstatic dancing, miraculous cures and the pursuit of wisdom personified as a divine woman". If this is the case, then it explains a great deal about the marked differences between the medieval confessions of Witchcraft in Europe proper and those of the British Isles.

Further Eastern aspects of the Goddess arrived in the form of Astarte, fertility goddess of Canaan and, as an integral part of Judaic faith, Lilith - the first wife of Adam but later relegated to the role of she-devil. She also appeared in the form of the Sumerian deity Ishtar and in Isis from ancient Egypt - all symbolising the mystical element of the Goddess which Michael Howard summed up by saying: "... this aspect of the feminine has always been rejected by patriarchal cultures whose sexual puritanism transformed it into a demonic symbol because they were incapable of handling the potent erotic energies associated with it."

Inspired by the fanatical teaching of the Spaniard Dominic de Guzman and his rabid hatred of heresy, in 1233 the Dominican Order's most infamous offspring was unleashed on an unsuspecting Europe - the Holy Inquisition. The Inquisition was a shock force of ecclesiastical butchers but prior to its inauguration, the first to fall foul of the ignominious Dominicans were the Cathars of the Languedoc area of France.

The Cathars accepted reincarnation and sought religious or mystical experiences at first hand, not through the offices of an intermediary, ie. a priest. They accepted the two irreconcilable principles of lightness and dark, spirit and matter, good and evil; how ever the Cathars recognised two gods, one a being of pure spirit and unsullied by the taint of matter, the other of material creation. That is to say that the world itself was intrinsically evil. In the eyes of Rome, the Cathars were guilty of a supreme heresy in regarding the material creation (for which Christ had died) as evil.

By 1200 there was also the fear that this particular brand of heresy could displace Catholicism and so Rome decided to eliminate the opposition. In 1209 an army of 30,000 knights and foot-soldiers swept into the Languedoc and the Albigensian Crusades began. The whole area was devastated and in Beziers alone, over 15,000 men, women and children were slaughtered. The hatred of de Guzman probably stemmed from his failure to convert the so-called heretics to the Catholic faith during his own zealous preaching in the area in 1204. By 1215 the Fourth Lateran Council decreed the total extermination of the Cathars (together with the Waldenses), on the charge of heresy. These atrocities lasted for nearly forty years, culminating in the famous the Siege of Montsegur, which finally fell after ten months of heroic defiance by the townspeople.

Dominic de Guzman died in 1221, two years before the inauguration of the Holy Inquisition but the thirst for blood in searching out heresy, spurred the Dominican Order on to greater refinements of brutal torture and execution. This time the target was the powerful and wealthy Order of the Poor Knights of Christ and the Temple of Solomon, or as they are more popularly known - the Knights Templar. The Order had had its roots in the Holy Land since 1118 and had gathered throughout the years immense wealth from initiates and even greater international power, through being involved in matters of high-level diplomacy.

By 1306 Philippe IV of France had decided to rid his land of the Templars but due to the fact that they were a highly trained, professional military force and much stronger than his own soldiers, he was unwilling to expel them by force. Also Philippe had his eye on the Templars' wealth and was not about to let it slip through his fingers. At dawn on Friday 13th October 1307, all Templars in France were arrested and subsequently accused of heresy. The Inquisition was in the forefront of the proceedings, their black cowls and white robes already recognisable as the uniform of death throughout Europe. The Grand Master of the Templars, Jacques de Molay, was cruelly roasted to death over a slow fire.

Although the battle cry was 'heresy' the true aim of the Roman Church was to eliminate any opposition as brutally and effectively as possible. And if the reader labours under the misapprehension that it was only non-Christians who suffered the penalties, they would be sadly mistaken. The Spiritual Franciscan friars, know for their gentleness and poverty, also attracted the wrath of the Holy See.

Rome was content that the Franciscans themselves lived at near-starvation level, but resented the charge that the clergy, even the pope himself, should follow Christ's example and put away material possession. As the acquisition of property and wealth was the main preoccupation of the bishops and cardinals at the time, the result was a declaration of heresy and excommunication was levelled against the order in 1315. The Church of Rome even went so far as to burn alive a number of these humble and dedicated monks in 1318. First hand experience of this barbaric treatment, however, did not prevent the Franciscans from lending a hand during the Witch-persecutions of a later age.

Once a victim had been denounced to the Inquisition there was no escape and it became a convenient way of settling old scores. A confessed Witch could implicate another by claiming to have seen the accused attending a sabbat but even if the accused confessed immediately on arrest, it was still necessary for her to undergo the prescribed torture - in case her first confession was false! The Inquisitors would not be denied their sport. Similarly in many cases the scribes taking down the confessions did not even bother to record the routine questions, and as the majority of confessions followed the same general pattern, their repetitiveness was held up as solid proof of the existence of Witchcraft.

The content of the confessions, suggested by the Inquisitors and eagerly admitted to by the victims under torture, were the fantasies of the Inquisition, not of the unfortunate women, who hoped that by confessing the pain would cease and they would, at least be strangled, rather than burned alive.

Informing on neighbours was encouraged and it was unnecessary for the informer to openly confront the accused. A man or woman could be denounced to the Inquisition without knowing who the accuser was, or even on what evidence they had been arrested. Once accused the victim had no rights. Witness were not identified and often their accusations were not even made known to the defendant. No witnesses were allowed to testify on behalf of the accused who was permitted no counsel, since the lawyer would be guilty of defending heresy.

England up to this period was fortunate in escaping much of the early barbarism and hysteria that threatened to envelope Europe. The concept of Witchcraft in the Middle Ages was one of almost benign acceptance in comparison with the 16/17th century 'conspiracy to overthrow the Christian God' and trafficking with the Devil. Local Witches were still consulted on matters of medicine and healing and it was only when they used their powers to the detriment of their neighbours that the law stepped in. Anyone found guilty of murder by Witchcraft received the death penalty, later reduced to banishment by William the Conqueror and later, during the reign of Edward I, a Witch who burned a neighbour's house was, herself, burned.

However, anyone had the right to claim trial by ordeal and *The Encyclopedia of Witchcraft and Demonology* cites a certain Agnes, wife of Odo, the earliest known person accused of sorcery, as being freed after the ordeal of grasping a red-hot iron (1209). If Agnes *was* left unscarred after grasping a red-hot poker, it is highly possible that she was a genuine Witch - or at least, had kinship with someone who was.

During this period of English history (1154-1485) the Plantagenets were on the throne and since legend claimed they were descended from the sorceress Mélusine, it was hardly likely that they were going to get themselves into a lather over the prospect of accusations of Witchcraft, except to use it as a political weapon against one another. Which they did with some frequency: they were not called the 'Devil's Brood' for nothing. Arrogant, flamboyant and colourful, the Angevin Kings gave England some of its most fascinating history. Between them they probably committed every crime in the book but they had one advantage over other European ruling houses - they were not slaves to Rome.

After the first excommunication, the ruling family and nobles became rather blasé over papal threats and tended to ignore them. Henry II came in for some papal flack during the Becket affair but it was his son John who managed to get the whole of England excommunicated for disobeying the edicts of Innocent III. In *The Pageant of England*, a quartet of books on the Plantagenets, Thomas B Costain tells us that "bans of excommunication which were hurled about in those days as freely as maledictions, flew back and forth ..." whilst Smith Minor observed that "the Pope made a law that no one might be born, get married or die, for the space of ten years". The English appear to have managed quite well without the offices of the Church of Rome, which suggests that many might, at this crucial time, have returned to the Old Religion for spiritual comfort.

In fact, so tolerant were the Plantagenats of Witchcraft that claims have been made that the higher Order in the land, The Order of the Garter, stems from Edward III's quick witted defence of his mistress, who had dropped her garter while dancing with the King. It has been suggested that the garter was a badge of membership of the Witch-cult and by the King placing the garter on his own leg, he effectively silenced the nobles and clergy who would have accused the Countess of Salisbury of being a Witch.

Upon examination the legend is not quite so preposterous as one might first think. Plantagenat ladies were not the shrinking violets that medieval ballads made them out to be and it would take considerably more than a falling garter to raise a blush. Historian Thomas Beaumont James even commented that only at the instigation of a king as powerful as Edward III could such a famous order of chivalry have as its symbol an article of ladies' underwear! So the Countess of Salisbury's garter must indeed have conveyed some significant message to the onlookers. It has also been claimed that the Black Book containing the original constitution of the Garter disappeared after Edward's death. Whether there is any truth in such stories will never be known but it is the stuff of which legends are made.

So powerful was the lure of the Goddess, that in England during the mid 1300s, special prominence was given to the Virgin Mary, who became more and more important in the popular devotion of the late Middle Ages, as is demonstrated by the art of the time. Was this a conscious move by the Church to elevate Mary to rival the Goddess in the minds of the people? Nearly all the important Pagan festivals had been incorporated into the church calendar, so why should the clergy be above exchanging the Earth Mother for Mary, the Mother of God? How many old churches contain a simple lady chapel to the side of the main altar? Mary was not divine and hardly warrants a separate altar, unless it was to offer an alternative Christian female image and Mary was the only suitable lady they had to hand.

Irrefutable proof that the Old Religion was still going strong in the Middle Ages is aptly demonstrated by the hundreds of representations of the Green Man and *Sheela-na-gigs* that adorn medieval ecclesiastical buildings. The master builders and architects might be gainfully employed to erect churches and cathedrals to the glory a Christian God, but their handiwork is indeed proof that their spiritual allegiance was to older ways. Most people today are familiar with that half concealed face, sprouting greenery like mutton-chop whiskers, peering out from carvings on wood and stone and his squatting female companion. Whatever interpretation historians and folk-lorists put on the figures, modern Pagans consider them to be representations of the Goddess and God.

At this stage we should also pay some attention to the use of magic in medieval Britain for it was not only local 'wise' women who practised the art of healing. Professor Kieckhefer claims that necromancy was a fairly common indulgence of those in the lower holy offices. Education was not for the poor and most young men attending medieval universities would automatically be ordained to the lower orders, thereby qualifying as an exorcist and receiving at the ceremony of ordination an exorcist's bible as a symbol of his office. And since many of the intelligensia's notions of magic came from classical graeco-roman literature, a great deal of personal interest in the occult could be cloaked with an aura of academic respectability.

Kieckhefer also suggests that if bored young monks could engage in necromancy, so too might priests and friars, for the common denominator between them all was a basic knowledge of the rites of exorcism, in addition to a passing acquaintance with astrology and many other forms of magic. The Professor cites recorded cases of such men having access to the infamous books on necromancy and, curious enough to try them out, being sternly chastised by their superiors.

Magic in the Middle Ages illustrates just how extensively magic was used in medieval times. Kieckhefe is not preparing a case for or against the existence of Witchcraft but investigating the use of magic and the attitude to the practitioners of it during that formative period of our history. He sees magic of the medieval period as a historical intersection between religion and science, and whereas demonic magic invokes evil resting on a "network of religious beliefs and practices, natural magic exploits occult powers within nature and is essentially a branch of medieval science".

We can see that magic blended primitive folklore with the academic learning pouring in from the Middle East; herbal remedies and thaumaturgic healing were now the province of peasant and educated alike, and if exhortation to God did not heal the sick, then the people turned back to the old ways and consulted the local wise woman for a cure. It was not unknown for Pagan magic to be used whilst invoking the assistance of some Christian saint, as is shown in the texts of the books of household management faithfully recorded in the Wolfsthurn and Munich handbooks.

It was during this period that medicine began to evolve as an independent science, although many of the cures still smacked of sorcery, and in setting up their infirmaries, the monks absorbed remedies from classical sources as well as traditional local methods. There were still many types of unofficial healers, including midwives, and A. R. Myers *(England in the Late Middle Ages)* observes that when peasants fell ill, they relied chiefly on "local women wise in the lore of herbs and other traditional remedies". However as the unprofessional rivals were always close to hand, the qualified physicians had every opportunity to cast the blame for their failures on the local Witch, thereby removing the opposition. This was all too readily accepted as throughout history, stories of magic and poison have gone hand in hand.

Love potions and poisons were amongst the magical remedies most in demand in both the French and English courts, and there are numerous recorded cases during this period that accuse members of the nobility of Witchcraft. In 1441 Eleanor Cobham, married to Humphrey, Duke of Gloucester was accused of having resorted to sorcery and Witchcraft in order to destroy the King and advance her husband to the crown. Humphrey had not been a popular figure during his brother Henry V's reign, and the accusations were politically motivated to discredit both the Duke and Duchess. So heavily did Duke Humphrey's enemies align themselves against the pair that Eleanor Cobham admitted most of the charges and was sentenced to public penance and perpetual imprisonment.

Witchcraft and the Sons of York is an illuminating document in which W. E. Hampton cited the various incidents involving charges of Witchcraft during that period. This *quasi*-legal method of upsetting a rival's apple-cart was used much the same as political scandal-mongering is used today. Most serious students of the Wars of the Roses are aware that accusations of Witchcraft and sorcery "were levelled, at times successfully, in every reign, whether of York or of Lancaster, against members of the ruling royal family. Two of York's surviving sons made accusations of Witchcraft against each other, whilst the third, Richard of Gloucester, levelled the accusation against the wife, the mother-in-law and the mistress of his brother Edward. (Neither did the Tudors hesitate to use the charge which Henry VIII used to destroy the most eminent of those Plantagenat descended nobles whose very existence the Tudors so resented.)"

In his famous *Encyclopedia of Witchcraft & Demonology* Rossell Hope Robbins erroneously states that Witchcraft came to England in 1563 but as we have seen, it was a continuance of the Old Religion, and was obviously still being practised strongly in rural districts. What Dr Robbins should have stated was that legalised Witch-hunting came to England in 1563.

Under the Tudors the the whole social and religious structure in England changed when Henry VIII brought about the dissolution of the monasteries, broke away from Rome and declared himself head of the Church of England. Strangely enough, although the people were no longer under allegiance to Rome, this period of history saw the start of the Witch-trials in this country which hitherto had escaped the lunacy being enacted in Europe. Using Witchcraft and heresy as an excuse, the Tudors climbed on the bandwagon of the trumped-up-charge.

Anne Boleyn was accused of being a Witch although she was executed for her alleged adultery; Mary burned a few heretics in an attempt to curry favour with Phillipe of Spain and get him into her bed; whilst Elizabeth removed a few more to put the Catholics back in their place and signed the Statute of 1563 resulting from "pressure of the clergy and made the Devil an acknowledged factor in the laws of the state."

With the accession of the House of Stuart to the throne (1603) open season was declared on practitioners of Witchcraft. Fitting the mood of the times, William Shakespeare's 'weird sisters' created an indelible caricature of Witches, which has persisted in theatrical adaptations ever since. Taken at face value, the three Witches are asked to do no more than divine Macbeth's bloodstained future, but the Bard added to the political, anti-Witch hysteria of Elizabethan England by creating in his own inimitable fashion, that *pot-pourri* of fiendish horror with which we are all familiar. Although much in dispute, the date given for the first appearance of *the Scottish play* is generally thought to be 1605-6, some three years after Elizabeth's death, but the characterisation no doubt reflected the public image of Witches as the 'secret, black and midnight hags' of the Elizabethan Witch-trials that had taken place during the preceding fifty years.

Not so famous, but even nastier, were the characters created by Ben Jonson for his *Masque of Queens*. The masque was performed on 2nd February 1609 at Whitehall Palace, with costumes and a stage design by Indigo Jones in such a lavish production that its estimated cost was £1400 for a single performance. The manuscript has survived intact, complete with Jonson's handwritten and elaborate stage settings, which was afterwards presented to Prince Henry. The theme of the masque was Evil being put to flight by Heroic Virtue; Jonson's reason for having an anti-masque featuring Witches (see Appendix III) was due to James I having written a book on Witchcraft and being obsessed by the subject. It does seem strange however, that in a climate of Witch-hysteria, a production such as *The Masque of Queens* should be staged for mere amusement. Unlike the rest of Europe, perhaps the English court felt itself immune from any danger and could afford to be amused by Jonson's unsavoury cast - comparable perhaps with today's alternative comedy extracting humour from AIDS. Those not affected by such happenings could afford to be smug at others' expense.

Even more terrible than fiction was the disturbing character of Matthew Hopkin, the Witch Finder General, whose specialty was to round up those accused of Witchcraft and subject them to the most humiliating public body-searches. In one year from 1645 to 1646 Hopkins "sent to the gallows more Witches than all the other Witch-hunters of England". Hundreds of women were dragged before a jeering mob and having had the clothes ripped from their backs, were made to undergo intimate searches for Witch-marks. No doubt modern psychiatry would have a name for Hopkin's condition but without fear of contradiction we may safely assume that his motivations were probably due more to sadistic leanings and greed than religious fervour.

The *stigmata diaboli*, or Devil's marks that were held up as evidence of Witchcraft, ultimately led to the deaths of hundreds of men, women and children. Warts, moles, old wounds, corns and birthmarks - common blemishes which adorn the bodies of *every human being in the world* - were considered marks of the Devil. Witchfinders were instructed to search in the most intimate places for such imprints, particularly the anus in men and the breasts and private parts of women. Not only were the accused stripped naked, every bit of hair was shaved from their bodies. The Witches' mark was just as damning and any small protuberance on the body could be classed as a devil's teat used for suckling familiars.

Pricking was another method of uncovering Witches and in addition to Hopkins there were plenty of other unpleasant characters about who set themselves up as roving 'finger men'. If the Witch-hunter ran a pin into the flesh of an accused Witch and the wound failed to bleed, this was taken as evidence of guilt. There are in existence today, pricking instruments with retractable pins that were used to chalk up the numbers of guilty parties and earn the Witch-finders their gruesome fees.

There is a recorded instance where one of the hapless women found a champion in a certain Lieutenant Colonel Hobson who witnessed a respectable woman being subjected to 'pricking'. The lady in question ... "in sight of all the people, he laid her body naked to the waist, with her clothes over her head, by which fright and shame, all her blood contracted into one part of her body." The Witch-finder stabbing with his pin produced no sign of bleeding but Hobson demanded that the woman be allowed to stand and that the pin be run into her thigh, which produced the required flow of blood to prove her innocence.

To correct a popular misconception, English Witches were not burned alive at the stake - the universal practice elsewhere, including Scotland. Under English law, burning was the penalty for *petit-treason;* with supportive documentary evidence of women being found guilty of poisoning an unwanted spouse who suffered this penalty. Nor were there mass executions like those carried out in France and Germany. There were probably no more than a 1000 people convicted and executed for Witchcraft in England but if we take away the pitiful minority who may possibly have committed murder, we are still left with a thousand innocent people dead as a result of religious bigotry.

By the time the throne passed to the House of Hanover in 1714 the Witch-hunts had burned themselves out. The last person to be executed for Witchcraft in England was Alice Molland in 1684 and the last indictment was against Jane Clerk in 1717 - but in this case, the lady got off. George II's Statute of 1736 repealed the archaic statute of 1604 but instead of abolishing the Witchcraft Act completely, it reversed it. No longer would the law punish Witches, it would only turn its attention to those who thought they were Witches!

It was not until the world had seen two world wars and genocide of equal magnitude that the Witchcraft Act was finally repealed in 1951. Nevertheless it would appear that the Old Religion HAD indeed survived, albeit in a degenerate form, well into the Late Middle Ages.

Chapter 5: The Devil To Pay

'Evil events from evil causes spring' wrote Aristophanes (BC448-380), providing a suitable banner headline under which to introduce the subject of Satanism.

In contrast to Witchcraft, it is questionable whether Satanism can be classed as a genuine belief system or whether it is merely another *quasi*-religious cult, established as recently as 1966 in America. Nevertheless, since the advent of the 'satanic child-abuse' allegations, it is a term that has discovered a new-found popularity within the media. Although judging from the use of the term, it is doubtful whether the journalists who juggle around with the phrase fully comprehend the implications of Satanism as it is understood by its handful of supporters.

The most infamous practice of all devil worship is still considered to be the black mass. Although according to most fictional accounts, a black mass was celebrated at every sabbat, there are no contemporary accounts of this in traditional Witchcraft. The term only became fashionable at the end of the 19th century in connection with Satanism and to quote Dr Robbins: No matter how titillating, all accounts of black masses (with one questionable exception) must be dismissed as unfounded speculation.

In the eyes of the Inquisitors, Witchcraft should parody Christianity and to emphasise the enormity of the blasphemy, they concocted the most amazing fantasies of how priests mixed semen with holy chrism oil, up-ended the cross, and enacted all manner of disgusting practices involving the host. *"Even from early times, the satanic mass was a literary creation borne out of questionable ecclesiastical minds for the destruction of their fellows,"* writes Robbins.

Man, Myth & Magic, however, contends that the ceremony referred to as the black mass is essentially a magical operation and bears little resemblance to the worship of Satan of popular imagination. Although there does not exist a single document describing the rites of a black mass at first hand, there are clues pointing towards rites which are 'quite divorced from Christianity or any other theology'. For example, it is known that in the 7th century the Church Council of Toledo denounced a 'Mass of the Dead' which was not designed to deliver the soul of a dead man from purgatory but to bring about the death of one who was living.

There is also the sinister 'Mass of St. Secaire' during which *a priest* performs the ceremony in a ruined church, his server is a woman with whom he has copulated, together with the usual trappings of a blackened host, water in which an unbaptized child has been drowned, etc. The outcome of this 'malignant' ceremony is the death of its victim, who wastes away by inches - *but it is not part of Witch-lore.*

The famous *Chambre Ardente Affaire* in 1679 brought rumours of the black mass to public attention for the first time, painting lurid pictures of frenzied priests sprinkling the breasts of a naked girl with blood from a newborn baby. The *Affaire* had all the trappings of a best selling novel and involved a poison ring, royal ladies-in-waiting, a favourite of the King, one of his mistresses, the Captain of the King's Guard and two rather unwholesome characters, namely *La Boss* and *La Voisin* who were subsequently burned as a result of their involvement in this *cause célebre.*

Suggestions of Satanism had already crept into the *Affaire* when two priests were accused of conducting black masses over the naked bodies of young women who were used for 'obscene ceremonial manipulations'. Under torture came confessions admitting to the sacrifice of children, white pigeons, and one admission of practising 'abominations with a big Easter candle'. A succession of unsavoury characters related an ever increasing catalogue of equally unsavoury stories until the whole *Affaire* began to get out of hand.

The most embarrassing revelation was that Madame de Montespan, mistress of Louis XIV, was the implementor of the satanic rites. Terrified of losing the King's affections to a younger woman, the lady had resorted to more diabolical means of disposing of her rival. The biggest problem that faced the investigating officers was the problem of how to stifle the most humiliating scandal of the century. Many low born incriminated in the *Affaire* were tortured and burned but none of the nobility were affected other than being banished from court. In 1709 Louis decided to destroy the records but fortunately for history, the Police Commissioner's notes escaped destruction.

Similarly, the Hell-Fire Club was probably the most famous band of devil worshippers in history and although the members parodied the rites of the Church, their ceremonies were more amoral than evil. The members were some of the leading politicians and intellectuals of the day, and amongst some the famous visitors to attend the meetings were Casanova, the Chevalier d'eon (of indeterminate sex) and Benjamin Franklin, the American statesman. Sir Francis Dashwood and his followers no more believed in the Devil than they believed in moderation and the Hell-Fire Club was, in fact, nothing more than a glorified brothel.

Founded on the ashes of a former club of the same name, it is alleged that the members 'in their bawdiness' excelled all the libertines of the reign of Charles II and not even the great Casanova was their equal. The original Hell Fire Club had drawn the attention of the authorities when the members had celebrated a mass on the body of a naked girl, stretched out on a bar-room table. The 'nuns' who provided the sexual favours were, during the Medmenham period of the Order of St Francis, not harlots, but respectable married women. Later, one of London's most notorious madams was requested to provide the girls for the "most licentious gathering of men and women who ever met to enjoy themselves on English soil". Although the Club parodied the rites of the Church as part of their ritual, they cannot seriously to be considered Satanists - they were there for the 'birds and the booze', and very little else.

The Hell-Fire Club delighted in shocking the more pure minded and scandal followed scandal. However it was not until the 19th century when the fervour surrounding Witchcraft had died away that a 'few wayward minds' created the black mass as is thought of today - as a service dedicated to the antichrist, Satan. Although some trace this back to the 18th century literary invention of the Marquis de Sade's most infamous fiction, *Justine*, in which the heroine herself relates:

... our libertine monks, to compound their impieties, wished Florette to appear at their nightly orgies in the same vestments which had brought her

so much veneration as the Blessed Virgin. Each one of them whipped up his filthy desires to commit the vagaries of his lusts with her in this costume. Excited by this first blasphemy, they counted other sacrileges for naught. The monks made this virgin strip and lie down flat on her belly on a big table. They lit holy candles and placed a statue of our Lord between her legs, and had the audacity to celebrate the most holy of our sacraments on the buttocks of this young girl.

At this horrible spectacle I fainted for I could not endure it. Father Serino saw me in this condition, and told me that in order to be humbled I had to serve, in my turn, as the altar. They grasped me and laid me where Florette had been. The sacrifice of mass was consummated. Severino seized the host, that sacred symbol of our venerable religion, and pushed it in the obscene entrance he used for his perverted pleasures, abusively pressing it in; then he ignominiously crushed it under the repeated lunges of his monstrous tool, and, shouting blasphemies, emitted the foul surges of the torrent of his lubricity over the very body of his Saviour ...

It is probably this fictional account of de Sade's, added to the factual account of the *Chambre Ardente Affaire*, which has provided every occult novelist and Christian fundamentalist with the standard format for a black mass. Anton Lavey states quite categorically: "No other single device has been associated with Satanism as much as the black mass. To say that the most blasphemous of all religious ceremonies is nothing more than a literary invention is certainly a statement which needs qualifying - but nothing could be truer." Lavey also affirms that the first commercial black mass was celebrated in 1666 by Catherine Deshayes or *La Voisin*, (the lady already mentioned above in the *Chambre Ardente Affaire*) and the "organised fraud perpetrated in these ceremonies has become indelibly marked in history as the true black mass."

Although Aleister Crowley has often been described as a Satanist and devil worshipper, C R Cammell, a personal friend of Crowley's refutes the charges that Crowley celebrated the black mass, an act of which he was so often accused. He says that ... "whether Crowley in his youth had ever performed that odious ceremony I do not know for certain. He has been accused of having done so in his Cambridge days, but on what authority is not clear. To me personally he denied it emphatically. He spoke always with the more profound contempt of such proceedings which he said were fit only for depraved schoolboys. When I knew Crowley such crazy travesties were not in his thoughts. Nor was it likely that they would have been; for Catholic rituals interested him no more than Catholic theology, and travesties thereof would naturally appear to him puerile. It was the far older Magic, the sorceries and Mysteries of ancient Egypt, Chaldea, Persia, India and Greece which interested him."

The confusion over Crowley's satanic identity appears to stem from several sources which have subsequently guaranteed that any book written by an occult investigator will, at some stage, fling in Crowley's influence just for good measure. Initially, Crowley developed his sexual-magical teachings from both his own research and experimentation which he later published in *The Book of Lies*. This publication attracted the attention of certain German occultists who accused Crowley of giving away the magical secrets of the *Ordo Templi Orientis*; it transpired that Crowley had worked the rituals out for himself by his own circumnavigatable route and he was subsequently invited to join the Order. Ever the adventurer, Crowley accepted.

The *Ordo Templi Orientis* claimed to work from the teachings of the Knights Templar (whose Order was disbanded at the beginning of the 14th century) expounding that sex could be used ritually or magically, embodying sex and yoga principles. Crowley assumed the magical name of Baphomet - the name of the figure which the Knights Templar were accused of worshipping and which had later been drawn by Eliphas Levi in the 19th century. This emblem has since been adopted by many occult practitioners and forms the insignia of the Church of Satan - hence its satanic connotations.

Levi depicted 'a pantheistic and magical figure of the Absolute', a diagram of the deity who represents the sum total of everything in the universe. The dual-sex, goat-figure contains symbols of the four elements, the head standing for fire, the wings for air, the scales for water, the legs for earth. The torch is a symbol of divine revelation; the pentagram of human intelligence; the white and black crescent moons for good and evil; the caduceus of the union of the sexes; the breasts and hands of maternity and toil.

At the outbreak of the First World War, Crowley introduced the O.T.O into America - groups claiming to continue the traditions of the O.T.O continue to exist throughout the USA, Scandinavia and Europe. There is much speculation surrounding sex-magic and because the O.T.O remains a 'closed' society, it was easy for occult investigators and fundamentalist propaganda to target their activities as satanic. A little known fact, however, is that the European O.T.O sued the publishers of a German translation anti-occult book for claiming that 'its members were mainly sado-paedophilians who were looking permanently for children whom they sexually abuse, etc'; a statement which did not appear in the English translation. It is doubtful whether any occult organisation would be willing to risk a high-cost legal battle if their activities were suspect but the O.T.O. went to court - they won the case!

When compiling *The Occult Census* in 1989, The Sorcerer's Apprentice had the foresight to include a section on Satanism, and even went so far as to invite British Satanists to define their own tenets of belief for public scrutiny along with other occultists. Unfortunately, their spokesman chose to submit an empty statement which did nothing to dispel the aura of mistrust and revulsion that surrounds the practice. Satanism IS controversial, but to open an article supposedly designed to redress the balance of understanding in the public mind, with the hackneyed statement that ... "Satanism is no longer a hook on which the unenlightened can hang their guilt-complexes" ... does not lessen the scepticism.

According to the 'proclamation', Satanists are concerned with reality and freedom of thought, summarising the satanic quest as 'We want to know.' They claim that two thousand years of being the scapegoat has left them on the defensive, when all they wish to know is what happens when the mortal body ceases to function and how to become more effective on earth. But, instead of taking a valuable opportunity to explain their doctrine, which was to be distributed to all interested official and academic departments, the reader was treated to a sermon of platitude which revealed nothing about the fundamental creed of British Satanism.

If Satanists are genuinely concerned about their image and wish to justify their existence in the public eye, why do they insist on maintaining a label that is widely accepted as fictitious Christian propaganda? It suggests that they enjoy the shock tactics that their beliefs provoke and even those claiming to adopt more ancient sources for their doctrines, overlook the fact that ancient folk did not regard deities normally identified with the underworld, death and the powers of darkness as personifications of ultimate evil. They were, and still are, regarded by occultists as essential aspects of the twin forces of creation and destruction that control the universe.

To parody Voltaire's timeworn phrase ... "that if the Devil didn't exist it would be necessary to invent him" ... illustrates exactly what the Satanists have created for themselves. One neo-satanic group claimed in an occult magazine that its own philosophy related to Thelema, the philosophy and magical system formulated by Aleister Crowley - and received a severe mauling in a subsequent issue from a British occultist for their presumption. However, since the aim of the *Malleus Satani* was not to defend or justify Satanism, but to illustrate why Satanism and Witchcraft are not synonymous with each other, it was obviously necessary to cast the research nets further afield.

There appears to be little sympathy for Satanists amongst other occult factions, some even going so far as to consign them to a 'spiritual kindergarten' and suggesting that those who advocate close links between Satanism and the Pagan movement, or that Satanists and Pagans join forces to combat attacks by fundamentalists, were either totally misguided or had motives which needed serious questioning. These responses spring from charges underlining the differences between the two belief systems in that modern satanic groups have always been critical of the neo-Pagan revival in their publications, and it has only been since the growth of the pagan movement that Satanist have sought any opportunity for discussion.

Michael Howard, writing in *Ocular Magazine* explains: "Modern Satanism is largely patriarchal with women taking a lesser role and often seen as 'altar fodder'. On a political level, many Satanists profess extreme right wing views ... some openly espouse neo-Nazi beliefs. The attitude of Satanists to the natural world takes the standard Christian line that it has to be dominated and controlled for the benefit of humankind. As one would expect from a philosophy which grew out of Churchianity, modern Satanism is conservative to the point of being reactionary and authoritarian in nature. For these reasons it is directly opposed to the beliefs professed by Pagans and Wiccans."

From a researcher's position it would seem that the existence of Satanism is confined to those seeking more unorthodox or illegal gratification but since *The Occult Census* showed that 4% of those taking part had a genuine interest in Satanism, objectivity demanded that the census organiser be asked for a clarification of modern Satanism and devil worship. Chris Bray gave the following viewpoint on the misconceptions surrounding satanic philosophy but suggested that contact be made with the Church of Satan in America for a broader view:

"People who call themselves Satanists tend to fall into two categories. Those who are using the title as an excuse for a club within which they can indulge their fantasies and excesses. These are the ones termed 'devil worshippers' by the press and are the usual idiots who seek notoriety beyond the value of their character or intelligence, and find exhibitionism a good vehicle for their ego. These fools will fantasise any amazing notion in order to gain a few extra column inches of fame and usually take their lead from the fantasies of the Christian fundamentalists themselves.

"In fact, devil worshippers are by qualification ALWAYS lapsed Christians for only a disenfranchised Christian would parody Christian theology. Usually devil worshippers are the illiterate products of a Christian culture and haven't the wit to see themselves as they are, let alone organise a pan-global attempt to undermine society. These are the kind of people who sniff glue, break into churches and desecrate tombs. In virtually every case, their simple minds leads them into conflict with the law on a small scale; more on a 'stumbling into' rather than as a planned operation. The media then dress the fools up with sinister motives and subversive intent and make their stupidity sound almost triumphal, thereby instilling a purely imaginary fear into the minds of ordinary folk.

"There are a small number of occult groups around, both in the UK and abroad, where something approaching a complete philosophy of Satanism has developed. The idea is a kind of Hedonism where individuals are not prepared to live life second hand and actively seek out and experience things which go beyond the norm. The highest aim of this kind of Satanism is Knowledge and so the constant thirst for knowledge can lead to great discoveries and insights.

"Devil worshippers are self-taught; self-generated and their silliness occurs sporadically throughout the UK - usually on monkey-see-monkey-do basis, following articles about occultism in the sensationalist press. Each cell of devil worshippers comprises of one self-styled leader and one or two 'thickie' followers, rarely having any connection with other groups, blossoming and subsiding with their leader's interest. It is true to say that devil worshippers keep out of the way of genuine occultists lest they reveal their ignorance and lack of genuine occult training. Hedonistic Satanists are much better organised and usually very creative and intelligent but their numbers are very few in number, as was revealed by *The 1989 Occult Census* which showed that only 4% of the sample of over 1000 occultists polled had any interest in Satanism. There is nothing in the philosophies or teachings of Hedonistic Satanism which Q.E.D. involve criminality.

Anton Lavey's observations are more to the point and less generous: "There are Satanists and there are nuts!" He also expresses his disdain over the pre-eminence given to self-styled, 'occult investigators' who appoint themselves authoritative status: "They obviously don't know the first thing about what I've written or what I advocate. If they'd read my books instead of just waving them in the air, they might know something about Satanism."

By comparison to British dissembling, LaVey's *Satanic Bible* offers a clear picture of established Satanism in the USA. LaVey at least has the courage of his convictions in stating quite openly that there is no altruism or love-thy-neighbour concept in the Satanic belief, except in the sense of helping other adherents on the Path to gain their desires by group energy. Satanism is a blatantly selfish, brutal religion. "It is based on the belief that man is inherently a selfish, violent creature, that life is a Darwinian struggle for survival of the fittest, that the earth will be ruled by those who fight to win the ceaseless competition that exists in all jungles ..."

Having formed the Church of Satan in San Francisco in 1966, LaVey based his doctrines on the reversal of worshipping the spirit and denying the flesh. Seeing the need for a church that would recapture man's body and carnal desires as objects of celebration and since the worship of fleshly things produces pleasure, then he would offer a temple of 'glorious indulgence' that would be fun for people. Realising that his ideas could not be mere philosophy, he recognised the need to form a religion - and to consecrate the newly established Church in the name of the Infernal. Since, he claims, there had always been a satanic underground, it was high time there was an organised satanic religion, practising openly.

In the Nine Satanic Statements, (Appendix II) LaVey's doctrine is revealed as indulgence instead of abstinence and the representation of vital existence, not spiritual pipe-dreams; wisdom overcoming self-deceit and kindness to those who deserve it, instead of ingrates. The Statements reverse the principle of turning the other cheek and demands vengeance, with total dismissal of psychic vampires. "Satan represents man as just another animal, sometimes better, more often worse than those that walk on all-fours, who, because of his divine spiritual and intellectual development, has become the most vicious animal of all."

This demonstration of political 'incorrectness' has brought in its wake charges of overt right-wing politics and neo-Nazism which are rejected by LaVey: "We aren't against Jews, Blacks, Whites ... We refuse to continue to compromise our standards to allow for stupidity and laziness! They have to be expected to come up to our standards rather than us lowering hurdles to suit them. If they can't, they should be told, probably for the first time in their lives; 'You know what? You're stupid! You're inferior!' instead of being protected from the effects of their incompetence. If a person is ethical, productive, sensitive, and knows how to conduct himself among human beings, fine; if he's an amoral parasite, he should be dealt with quickly and cruelly."

Remaining true to the principle of finding out about a 'pine tree from a pine tree', the obvious step *was* to make contact with the group originally responsible for the formulation of the whole modern satanic movement. Blanche Barton has been involved with the Church of Satan since the early 1980's and works as an administrator for the organisation, as well as having written several books on the Church and its founder. As the author of *The Secret Life Of A Satanist,* Blanche Barton doesn't try to hide her enthusiasm or support for her mentor but she does give a clear insight into the development and daring of a man, who through a charismatic personality and the ultimate style in showmanship, has revolutionised religious thinking in a country the size of America.

In explaining her own commitment to the satanic creed, she explains: "My use of the metaphor of Satan, as opposed to the Mother Goddess or Jesus Christ or some other such image, inspires and enlivens me because he is the strong, defiant, rebellious iconoclastic anti-hero, who is at once my Father, my Mentor, my Lover, and my Brother. The appeal for me *must* be sexual (something I do not feel toward another female image or toward a eunuch on a cross); Satan is ruthlessly demanding, compelling, obsessive, intoxicating ...

"He is a wicked and perverse tormentor who challenges me to surpass my own expectations of myself; he is the ever-lusting Pan, greedy for life; he is Prometheus, the one who defied his brother-Gods by stealing the creative Fire for Man. For me, the methaphorical representations of the Dark One throughout history have always been more interesting, complex and invigorating. Magic comes from the interaction between the Yin and the Yang, the complete manifestations of both. As Mr LaVey gets into in *The Satanic Witch*, the more completely we manifest our Apparent Selves, the more attuned we become to our Demonic Cores as well. And you can then utilize the power of both within you."

Anton LaVey himself explains the use of 'the metaphor of Satan' in his biography, which may come as a surprise to many: **"We don't worship Satan, we worship ourselves using the metaphorical representation of the qualities of Satan.** Satan is the name used by Judeo-Christians for that force of individuality and pride within us. But the force itself has been called by many names. We embrace Christian myths of Satan and Lucifer, along with Satanic renderings in Greek, Roman, Islamic, Sumerian, Syrian, Phrygian, Egyptian, Chinese or Hindu mythologies, to name but a few. We are not limited to one deity, but encompass all the expressions of the accuser or the one who advocates free thought and rational alternatives ... we are living in a culture that is predominantly Judeo-Christian, so we emphasize Satan."

Using the misnomer 'Witch' for his female followers, Anton LaVey openly declares that since women are undeniably different from men, a woman's power lies in her exploiting her unique attributes. With the publication of *The Satanic Witch* (which brought howls of protest from the feminist league with public book burnings and pickets at stores) the arch-Satanist gave his woman's guide to enchantment - on how to unashamedly use artifice, wile and guile to get whatever they desire. LaVey prefers the more seductive image of a Witch as an enchantress, one who fascinates, rather than the Feminist/Wiccan revision who 'practice more male-bashing than magic'.

His views are undiluted chauvinism and he has no qualms in admitting to being a confirmed misogynist with little positive response about the effects of feminism. "Feminism negates and inverts the natural male/female interchange. There's a magnetic interaction between men and women that can be exploited for magical reasons, like a perpetual motion machine ... In Satanic ceremonies, it's the interplay between the dominant priest and the receptive female altar ... The feminists have eliminated avenues of power over men that women have had for centuries."

"I think Mr LaVey's posture as a self-confessed misogynist should be clarified," added Blanche Barton. "If you read his article on the subject that is included in *The Devil's Notebook*, you'll see that he intends his confession to be taken as something of a literary conceit - meaning, the reason he claims to hate women is because he is so fascinated by their power; that he realises they can do things he cannot, and that he feels somewhat in awe of them. And that fascination and admiration makes him vulnerable, which he resents. It's a strong admission to be man enough to make.
"The introduction to *The Satanic Witch* also makes it clear that he acknowledges that woman have always been painted the Devil's best allies because they can do things that men can never do. That a woman who is bold enough, confident enough, and sharp enough to use her sexuality *and* her brains to get want she wants is probably the most powerful entity on earth. That's why he wrote the book. My personal experience of Mr LaVey has indeed borne his attitude out. I don't know if any of this answers your question about 'altar fodder' or not, but that is why I can only be a Satanist."

The Satanic disdain for those who call themselves 'Pagans' or 'Wiccans' are similar to many of the claims made by Pagans against Satanists: "... and really has been explained in *The Satanic Bible*," says Blanche Barton. "They are using the tools of Satan and expect the benefits but are afraid to give the Devil his due. They claim use of all the arts that have always been considered heretical, the realm of 'black magic', yet want to dress it up in white-light and gossamer. If they are going to stand in defiance of hypocrisy and Christianity, why not call themselves Satanists? Why are they so afraid of the dreaded 'S-word'?
"During the recent hysteria, in fact, the 'Wiccans' were only too happy to align themselves with the Christians in saying, "Yes, indeed - Satanists do sacrifice animals and babies. Don't you dare confuse us with those rotten Satanists." The books defining our beliefs have been on the shelves for 25 years now and yet they still misrepresent what we stand for. As much as they want to yell that they're not Satanists, the public really doesn't care. When they fan the flames of hysteria, they are ultimately fueling a wildfire of bigotry and

censorship that would make no such distinctions. It's because of that kind of hypocrisy that many Satanists tend to think of those who must call themselves Pagans as 'the last Christians'."

Because of the 'negative social attitude problems' identified with satanic involvement, it may come as a surprise to discover that there are such things as 'sins' and a 'code of practice' (Appendix II) within Satanic doctrine. The basic difference is that where other religions develop sins that people can't avoid, the Church of Satan considers a number of things sinful that people could avoid - if they are willing to work at the remedy.

Top of the list is **Stupidity**, which is considered to be the cardinal sin of Satanism - ignorance is one thing, but society thrives increasingly on stupidity which is unacceptable to the Satanist.

Pretentiousness is on an equal footing with stupidity since empty posturing can be most irritating and isn't applying the cardinal rules of Lesser Magic.

Solipsism, or absolute egoism is the theory that the only knowledge possible is that of oneself; projecting your reactions, responses, and sensibilities onto someone else who is probably far less attuned than you is a mistake, since you expect the same courtesy, consideration and respect in return.

Self deceit is another cardinal sin which should only be entered into for fun and with awareness - but then it's not self-deceit!

Herd conformity comes next: it's allright to conform to a person's wishes, if it ultimately benefits you - only fools go along with the herd, letting impersonal entities dictate form.

Lack of perspective - you must never lose sight of who and what you are, and what a threat you can be, by your very existence; always keeping the wider historical and social picture in mind is an important key to both Lesser and Greater Magic.

Forgetfulness of past orthodoxies is one of the keys to brainwashing people into accepting something as 'new' and 'different', when in reality it's something that was once widely accepted but is now presented in a new package.

Counterproductive pride: pride is great up to the point you begin to through the baby out with the bathwater. The rule of Satanism is: if it works for you, great. When it stops working for you, when you've painted yourself into a corner and the only way out is to say, "I'm sorry, I made a mistake, I wish we could compromise somehow," then do it.

Lack of aesthetics is the physical application of the balance factor and is important in Lesser Magic; it's not what's supposed to be pleasing - it's what is. Aesthetics is a highly personal thing, reflective of one's own nature, but there are universally pleasing and harmonious configurations that should not be denied.

Anton Lavey is equally as scathing about those jumping on the satanic bandwagon and issues a strongly worded warning to those new to the Realm of Darkness. "There are unethical individuals out there who will prey upon you; claim to teach you how to become a Great Black Magician overnight; who will promise instructional fellowship and activities with 'True Masters'; who may claim unverifiable links with the Church of Satan, or other such lineage. Save your money

"When someone claims to have a direct line of communication with Satan, watch out! Look out for jargon and secrets that only the 'initiated' can be privy to. Once you're processed through the lengthy and strictly-enforced 'degree' system, you'll discover there are really no answers, just more gobbledygook. If they have something worthwhile to say, they'll say it. If they don't, they'll pretend they do anyway."

Most pseudo-satanic groups have a short lifespan but they can do untold damage in the interim, particularly to the wallet and self-esteem. "Be wary of the 'You probably aren't smart enough to join us' approach. The only way you can prove them wrong is by joining! From the first material you get, you feel you have to prove and defend yourself. Don't be fooled by big words, nice typing and/or fancy paper ... and plenty of it. True Satanism builds the ego, it doesn't tear it down ... Beware of cults offering sex orgies and drugs, or killing animals in the name of Satan. These are NOT part of Satanic practices. Use common sense. Don't let someone take advantage of you for his or her own perversity: examine motives carefully."

LaVey is nevertheless anxious to point out that not all groups are counterproductive to Satanism as a movement; there are many which are productive, supportive branches of the Church of Satan. Like various divisions of the same army, these distinct Orders may emphasize one Satanic image over another, but they are all aligned, in communication and working towards the same goals. But, he insists, you must be prepared to sort the truth from the misinformation. Don't be fooled by self-declared 'Masters' whether they're wearing white robes or black. They are attempting to misdirect and subvert whatever you've developed in the way of ego or identity. If it seems to be too good to be true - it probably is!

Whether one accepts the teachings of Anton LaVey's Church of Satan or rejects them out of hand, it must be recognised that the man is honest about the path of worship his followers tread, and there may have been far more respect for U.K. satanic belief if the proclamation made in *The Occult Census* had expressed similar sentiments to those of *The Satanic Bible*. Whilst it is appreciated that Satanism may mean something quite different to other sects, 'Satanism Defined - by Satanists' as it appeared in *The Occult Census* does nothing to enhance the satanic image. It suggests that it is not only orthodox religions who are aware of the 'insecure foundations of their own dogma' - British Satanism appears to be on an unsound footing too.

Chapter 6:   Sex and the Devil

o how did two completely separate religions become so inextricably interwoven, to such a degree that many aspects have become inseparable in the public mind? As we have seen, one was the older more liberal worship of a Godhead in the form of the Earth Mother and her consort, the Horned God; on the other hand there was the newer, more austere patriarchal Satanism with its multitudinous sources.

Having absorbed most of the Old Religion's festivals into the Church calendar, Rome was in the position of either having to operate in tandem with the many other minority groups springing into existence in medieval Europe, or suppress them by the process of complete annihilation. In *Sex, Dissidence and Damnation*, Jeffrey Richards presents an authoritative study of six medieval groups which the Church broadly fitted into religious (Jews, Witches, heretics) and sexual (homosexual, prostitutes and lepers) categories, with one common denominator - *perverted sex.*

It was this stereotype of the 'lustful deviant' closely linked with the Devil that was used to demonize them all, and to be identified by the Church as being part of a world-wide satanic conspiracy aimed at undermining Christianity in the 11th century. During the Middle Ages there was a deep entrenchment of an alternative morality to that required by the clergy, which Richards identifies as a morality of pre-Christian tribal and peasant society, in which sexual life was unrestricted by religious dogma. Marriages of the time were often informal affairs and easily dissolved; and if the sexual act was believed to be innocent and pleasure derived from it, then it was not disagreeable to God.

Needless to say, these Pagan attitudes were anathema to the Church who associated all illicit sex with the Devil and subsequently there were certain elements of Paganism which defied Christian absorption, particularly the fertility cults. In Richards' opinion, overt Paganism with strong overtones of magic continued to exist and to be fought by the Church and state until the ninth century. Indeed early medieval laws contain regular references to Witchcraft, though not, as Richards' points out, as devil-worship.

Seen in its true perspective, it is possible to trace the Christian allegations made against Witches and heretics as being the same as those made by classical writers against the early Christians - incest, infanticide, sodomy, cannibalism and orgies. In fact, according to medievalist Norman Cohn it was standard practice to brand ALL dissident religious groups with the most heinous of crimes, and by the Middle Ages a common stock of slanders existed in the classical texts for the monastic writers to plunder and redeploy. Such texts were regularly lifted verbatim and applied to the new dissident groups.

Professor Cohn claimed that this familiar propaganda technique was taken further by early Christian writers - thereby creating a convincing but deceptive image of an overall satanic conspiracy. It was also his contention that *devil-worshipping Witches had no existence in popular culture, indeed no existence at all outside the fevered imaginations and paranoid delusions of a group of medieval clerical intellectuals*. He also traces the development of the satanic Witch-cult in the cumulative process of propaganda by which ALL religious dissidents were demonized and its irony lies in that many of the heretical groups branded as devil-worshippers were more pious and chaste than their accusers.

Once the pattern of satanic activities was established as part of the propaganda machine, it could be regularly amended and extended to include any other unspeakable acts that came to light in classical sources. The recurrence of the same ideas in the accounts of the persecutions of the Jews, Waldenses, the Cathars and the Knights Templar all demonstrate identical allegations of devil worship and sodomy, which became synonymous with all forms of lechery, sexual deviance, leprosy and magic.

The satanic myth first appears in the 9th century AD, gathering momentum until the 15th century AD when the Devil appears as a fully developed satanic entity. The majority of modern fundamentalist charges against Witchcraft stem from the Papal Bulls of medieval Europe, when a considerable amount of documentation was compiled from previous classical literature on the subject of perversion and transposed to cover both Witchcraft and heresy.

Evidence was usually given of the licentious heretical practices which involved kissing the Devil under his tail - the kiss of shame that was so vividly described during later proceedings at a Scottish trial, when one of the accused claimed that: "The Devil caused all the company to come and kiss his arse, which they all said was cold like ice." This obscene kiss featured amongst the accusations levelled at both the Waldenses and the Knights Templar, and it is Michael Howard's suggestion that the origins of the 'kiss of shame' may have been introduced into Europe by initiates of Saracen occultism, although he has never heard of its use within modern Witchcraft, despite fictional accounts so frequently quoted. It also was around this period that tales began to spread of the Jewish community condoning the ritual murder of Christian children as part of their rites.

Although the Church pursued Witches as heretics from the 9th century, the Witch-trials on a grand scale happened after 1300. Jeffrey Richards suggests that these can be linked to the climatic change in Europe around that time which unleashed a succession of harvest failures, flood, famine and plague. The cause of this was blamed on Witches and heretics who had brought the wrath of God down on the populace, and their guilt could only be expurged by casting them into the flames. Added to the various political scenarios that existed at the time, and finding it expedient to remove such opposition as the Cathars and Templars, the Church subjected Europe to an ecclesiastical spring clean.

Richards concludes his chapter on Witches by conclusively rejecting the idea that devil-worshipping Witches really existed, and that those Witches who continued to follow the old Pagan tradition were targeted as unholy conspirators. "There may have been a few stray eccentrics who did worship the Devil but the satanic conspiracy was the creation of Catholic intellectuals, theologians, and jurists who merged ancient folk beliefs, learned magic, and rural witchcraft, emphasised the role of sex and posulated the aim of destroying Christendom." The satanist Witches of the late Middle Ages were, then, the ultimate scapegoats, an invented minority, a composite image of evil, ready-made for application to anyone who disagreed with Church dogma, which was fed into the public consciousness until it bore horrific fruit in the Witch hunts of the 16th and 17th centuries.

Adding fuel to the growing satanic conspiracy propaganda, the Dominican, Thomas Aquinas (1227-74) penned *Quaestiones Quodlibetales* which influenced eccliastical thinking on Witchcraft of that period and laid the foundation for the ensuing persecutions. Even as late at 1879, Pope Leo XIII decreed that all Catholic clergy should 'take the teachings of Aquinas as the basis of their theological position' and Sprenger and Kramer, co-authors of the *Malleus Maleficarum*, quoted him as one of their principle authorities. Aquinas too, seemed to have been preoccupied with the sexual habits of the Devil and according to his reasoning, what a demon was capable of doing with stolen semen as a means of artificial insemination would be the envy of any modern gynaecologist!

The Witch-persecutions that engulfed Europe for almost 500 years were the product of religious hysteria, born out of the fear of competition. The Christian Devil had been created for them out of Old Testament translations; he could be identified with the the horned deities of older religions and since the female aspect of the Goddess reflected Rome's dislike of, and belief in the corrupting influence of women, it was easy to pronounce the Craft as being devil infested.

The most excessive example of this attitude is to be found in one of the most damning work on Witchcraft - *Malleus Maleficarum* (*The Hammer of Witches* first published in 1486) which ran into fourteen editions during the next forty years. Although it has long been accepted that there is not one grain of truth in the *Malleus Maleficarum*, this perverted brainchild of two more Dominicans, Jacobus Sprenger and Heinrich Kramer, became the irrefutable Papal approved gospel of execution and torture throughout Europe, ultimately claiming an estimated 13 million victims. Jeffrey Richards' defines it as a work of 'pathological misogynism and sex-obsession'.

The Folio version used here is based on the translation by the Rev. Montague Summers (hence his reputation as an expert on the Craft), with an Introduction by Pennethorne Hughes who describes it as "a textbook of procedure: an official blueprint for the suppression of an underground movement against the Christian structure of medieval society ... Extermination must be careful but ruthless ... together with the means to extract confession and effect punishment. It expressed terror and authorised extermination."

The *Malleus Maleficarum* in its original form makes for difficult reading and Hughes shies away from including passages of the tortures and executions, by claiming that such 'details of human torture and degradation are best confined to medical textbooks and under-the-counter sadism'. Even in its abridged form, however, the Folio edition still gives a good indication of the Dominicans' preoccupation with sexual matters. Their fiction of sexual encounters with demons and incubi, and the methods of exacting confessions from their victims, rank with the rather excessive fantasies and sado-masochistic daydreams of de Sade rather than Papal law.

The Witch-trials took common, everyday occurrences and magnified them out of all proportion to illustrate the manner in which the Devil's disciples served him. Failure of crops, sick cattle and even freak weather conditions were blamed on Witchcraft. St Augustine had been banging on about the sins of the flesh and chastity became THE Christian virtue. All of which went against the grain for the average man and woman who had a normal Pagan appetite for fornication. Uta Ranke-Heinemann in *Eunuchs for Heaven* maintains that the church fathers were homosexuals who de-sexed themselves and then set about de-sexing the rest of humanity, with Augustine piling on the agony by declaring that any marriage consummated for pleasure's sake was a mortal sin - the act of fornication would cast the participants into the fires of Hell.

Eunuchs for Heaven also illustrates how easy it was for the *Malleus Malifecarum* to prey upon the age-old sexual fears of emasculation. Children born under suspicious circumstances were claimed to have been conceived through intercourse with incubi, rather than by the services of a lover. Any child that was particularly ugly or carried some deformity was claimed to have been sired by the Devil. Abortions and miscarriages were blamed on Witchcraft and a man might be unable to perform his marital obligations due to drink (or illness) but it was an ego-proof claim that the fault was due to spell casting.

The authors of the *Malleus Maleficarum* also claimed that all Witchcraft came from carnal lust 'which is in women insatiable" and "all wickedness is but little to the wickedness of a woman'. In view of this ecclesiastical misogyny, it is not surprising that medieval woman clung firmly to her ancient faith which placed male and female at level pegging. The Church knew how to threaten a man's masculinity, and held over him the constant risk of a wife, daughter, sister or mother succumbing to carnal temptation with demons; every female member of his family was a potential danger to his manhood.

Open air sex has always been a fairly popular pastime in rural areas and the less densely populated Middle Ages offered hundreds of pastoral bowers for lovers to meet. As many a girl has found to her cost, there is no animal fleeter of foot than the adulterous male on the brink of discovery. Might those unfortunate ladies who were discovered ...

... lying on their backs in the fields and woods, naked up to the very navel, and it had been apparent from the disposition of those limbs and members which pertain to the venereal act and orgasm, as also from the agitation of their legs and thighs, that, all invisibly to the bystanders, they had been copulating with incubus devils ...

... be merely suffering from the embarrassment of being caught *in flagrante delicto*? If her lover had taken off like a stag, the poor girl, with skirts flung over her head, would be thrashing helplessly about, and be reduced to ashes for a few moments of casual fornication.

There is little doubt that the Old Religion disintegrated during the Middle Ages, but whether it managed to descend as low as the Church and the Witch-finders would have us believe is quite another matter. Nearly all the information relating to Witchcraft in medieval Europe comes from the records of Witch-trials and since most of the confessions were extracted by torturous means, there can be no equation between truth and pain-racked fabrication. All the confessions, from the beginning of the persecutions in the 13th century to the early 18th century, smack of coercion.

Obviously the fertility/sexual aspects of the Witch-cult offended Church elders, exactly as they do today, but the English laws of the Early Middle Ages only imposed a penance on the offender, or clapped them in the stocks to be pelted with refuse at their neighbours' leisure. Missing from English trials, however, were the lurid descriptions of sabbat orgies which seemed to be the staple diet of French examinations. Perhaps English judges were less interested in the sexual habits of the accused than their French counterparts. And contrary to popular belief, the followers of traditional Witchcraft did not dance naked in open air rituals - this modern aspects of the Craft hails from sunnier climates than ours.

Possibly by the late Middle Ages the magical powers of many coven leaders had degenerated to such a degree that, in order to keep their influence, Pagan gatherings developed more orgiastic leanings. The sabbat was a time of ritual sharing, accompanied by chanting, incense burning and dancing - later parodied by the love-ins of hippy culture. The legends surrounding the 'free-love' of the 1960s stemmed not so much from debauchery, but from the desire to shake off repression and inhibitions; which may well have been the creed of the medieval Witch who, prior to the Church interfering, had no inhibitions to shed over the natural act of procreation.

It would be easy to dismiss as fabrication the whole scenario of sexual athletics attached to the Craft if it were not for the findings of Margaret Murray. Just how much of Dr Murray's research is reliable, is difficult to gauge but in an article on modern witchcraft, Robert Graves endorsed that 'three of four covens seemed somehow to have survived in England when Dr Murray's sympathetic reassessment of organised witchcraft made a revival possible'.

The charges of devil worship that surrounded the participants of a Witch gathering, were based on a belief that members of the coven paid homage to, and had sexual relations with, the Devil in the guise of a goat. It has been suggested that the male participant of the gathering who represented the Horned God (wearing a goat-mask or the antlers of a stag), would be called upon to perform the necessary sexual services required of a decayed fertility rite. Margaret Murray drew attention to the welter of documentary evidence that existed concerning the experiences of copulating with the Devil; suggesting that the stories were not hallucinatory but based on fact.

According to Murray's reports, sexual encounters with the Devil were not pleasurable; the women found it painful due to the huge dimensions of the penis and the semen being icy cold. The statements were the same from young girls to sexually experienced women - the Devil was a 'chilly individual with a large and pain-inflicting organ'. If this were indeed the case, and with the growing number of women attending the meetings, Dr Murray also suggested that it would have been necessary for the 'acting God' to adopt some form of artificial sex aid, larger than that of a normal male (for the recipient would expect 'different propensities' from the God), which squirted a cold liquid into the vagina for greater realism. Faced with the prospect of having sex with a number of women from maiden to crone, it would have been necessary for him to raise more than enthusiasm for the job. A daunting task even for a young fellow with a healthy libido, for the Horned God (real or not) could not be seen to shrink from the task.

Of course, there is no way of knowing how much of this is factual or if indeed any of it be true. Testimony and evidence from the Witch-trials would have circulated amongst the better educated and filtered down through gossip until everyone in the community would have known what Witches were SUPPOSED to do at their sabbats. Did certain groups parody the old Witch-cult for entertainment? Whether true or not, the orgiastic cavortings of popular belief found a firm hold in the public mind and has provided immeasurable 'evidence' for fundamentalist and fiction writer alike ever since. Chris Bray also added that since any quotation of 'facts' derived from the Witch-trials are based on Inquisition records which were simply substantiations of premeditated prejudice of the court, there is no evidence to suggest that Witches impersonated the devil at any time; and as the devil stereotype does not exist in Paganism such beliefs are doubly erroneous.

There is always the reverse side of the medal and it is not unreasonable to assume that there were those who remained faithful to the true path, their diligence keeping the lamp burning through the long nightmare of persecution and humiliation. Probably a few adherents did manage to keep the Craft alive in its traditional form, away from the corrupting influences, but this can never be proved, for in truth, no written records exist to support a claim of Hereditary Witchcraft . Robert Cochrane belonged to the Hereditary Craft and tells of a family tradition that his great-grandfather was Grand Master for the whole of Warwickshire and Staffordshire. Nevertheless, he was forced to write in 1964-5 that: "The old Craft is nearly dead. Various groups of people call themselves witches, but this in many cases is an excuse for high jinks and tawdry orgies ..."

Three years after the Witchcraft Act was repealed in 1951, Gerald Gardner published his famous work *Witchcraft Today*, the book that started the neo-Pagan movement and gave birth to the Gardnerian

Tradition. A retired civil servant, Gardner revealed the existence of a definite Witch cult, similar to the one suggested by Margaret Murray in the 1920s, following his initiation into a coven in the New Forest. In 1959, he published his second book, *The Meaning of Witchcraft*, in which he reiterated his statements about the 'healthy natural religion of Wicca', as he called the cult and set out to prove that Wicca had indeed been an established religion in these islands in pre-Christian times.

The aspect of Wicca which appealed most to the tabloid press was the fact that rituals were conducted with an entirely nude assembly, who engaged in ritual flagellation and when performing The Great Rite, two members of the coven actually carried out sexual intercourse in full view of the coven members. Needless to say, that from the media's point of view, any whiff of Witchcraft suggesting thirteen naked bodies pelting around a makeshift altar, followed by mass fornication conjured up pictures of the old style Witch-gatherings with their attendant Devil.

To the many who accept Gardner's theories, he is considered a 'brilliant scholar and a much maligned individual' but in *Man, Myth & Magic*, Frank Smyth suggests that in the absence of any concrete evidence, there is a strong case for believing that Gardner invented the modernised cult of Wicca to satisfy his own sense of the esoteric. His rituals were far more heavily based on sex than others practised at the time, and Smyth concludes that it is reasonable to suppose that Gardner's sexual whims were gratified by the religion he had created. Francis King in *Ritual Magic in England* pulled no punches in accusing him of being: "A sado-masochist with both a taste for flagellation and marked voyeuristic tendencies."

In later years, the Gardnerian Tradition was eclipsed by the Alexanderian cult, led by Manchester born Alex Sanders and his wife, Maxine. The Alexandrians continued the Gardnerian practice of working naked, or 'sky-clad' and were far more geared to cope with the attendant publicity that their leader courted. In fairness, no one considered the late Alex Sander's powers as affectation - it was his overt dedication to tasteless showmanship that non-Alexandrians found offensive. In an open letter to several Pagan magazines (1991), Patricia Crowther reminded readers that Sanders had been responsible for some of the most adverse publicity ever aimed at the Craft during the 1960s and did more to harm embryonic Paganism than anything its enemies could have invented.

With the publication of two books featuring the couple (*King of the Witches* by June Johns and *Maxine, the Witch Queen*) the popular concept of sexual activity playing an important role in Witchcraft was as strong as ever. With the usual photographic compliment of nude ceremonies, one book described an occasion when a woman friend was ceremonially blindfolded and strapped to a table, whilst the High Priestess assaulted her through the offices of a wooden dildo. This bizarre travesty was declared to be part of the third degree ceremony although one of the Wiccans helping with the author's research suggested an over-active imagination, whilst another claimed that it set a precedent in the annals of modern Witchcraft!

To those outside the Craft, modern Wicca under its trappings of a rejuvenated ancient fertility cult, was merely an excuse for sexual excess, and there seems to have been very little done to correct this impression. Robert Cochrane remarked that: "There had been no cause for a fertility religion in Europe since the advent of the coultershare plough in the 13th century," but the public and of course the Church, still preferred to see Witchcraft as being inextricably bound up with unbridled sex and devil worship.

When these and similar books were published during the late 1960s and 70s no one realised the serious repercussions that would boomerang against the occult community twenty years later. Much of the information contained in the books was later plagiarised to support the anti-occult propaganda of the present day. Modern satanic survivors cite the background information to give credence to their own stories and then offer the Sanders' books as proof of actual satanic happenings. One example is the exact re-hash of being acclaimed a Queen of the Witches at a vast open air ceremoney. Another was the use of the term *fith-fath* which Alex Sanders had used to describe a small image made of clay or plasticine to represent a person on whom a spell is to be cast; four years later, fundamentalists were describing the same images used for the same purpose.

However, according to Peter Elliott, editor of *ORCRO Magazine*, all of them have got it wrong: *fith-fath* is a Gaelic term for an invisible spell and nothing to do with dolls, clay or otherwise. What Peter does find interesting is, that before Sanders used the expression, the term was almost unknown; the only people to continue to bandy it about as the name of a wax or clay spell image have been Christian self-styled 'experts'.

The satanic survivor stories are indeed remarkable; one alleges that she was the Queen of the Witches of Europe and the mistress of the Chief Satanist. Hopping blithly from satanic temple to Witch coven, the satanic survivor was privileged to meet Lucifer himself in person the night she was crowned Queen of the Witches! The entire fictional scenario would be laughable if it were not for the fact that the stories are considered credible by certain fundamentalist Christians and used as proof to support the allegations of 'satanic child abuse'.

But what of the rites carried out by Witches in pursuit of their belief? Many of these have been cited by fundamentalists as a clear demonstration of perversion within the Craft and it is the initiation ceremonies that have aroused the greatest speculation in the minds of outsiders. Reports of binding and scourging of an initiate for purification purposes would be considered highly erotic by those with sado-masochistic tendencies and no doubt has attracted the wrong sort of interest in the Craft. However, since some groups remain robed, whilst others work naked, the initiation obviously differs from coven to coven, depending on whether they are of Gardnerian, Alexandrian or Hereditary Tradition.

Mike A. an experienced occultist, with a broad knowledge of the historical aspects of the Craft, suggests the possibility that the New Forest coven (to which Gardner was initiated) used ritual flagellation. He is, however, more inclined to believe the theory that Gardner WAS a sado-masochist who enjoyed being tied up and whipped by nubile priestesses, and that is why binding and scourging played such a prominent role in Gardner's original coven. Mike also feels that too much emphasis has been placed on this aspect which has distorted the conception of initiation in the public mind, especially as it has been phased out from most modern Wicca. (In *King of the Witches*, Alexandrian initiates received forty strokes on the buttocks from a silver whip with thongs of embroidery silk.)

Scourging plays no part in Hereditary/Traditional Witchcraft and neither does the famous Five Fold Kiss or Salute, which is bestowed by the High Priestess or Priest of sky-clad covens on the feet, knees, genitals, breasts and lips of new members. Since members of the Hereditary Craft remained robed, the kiss of welcome is placed on both cheeks of the initiate, after he or she has pledged a simple oath of allegiance to the Goddess. No doubt there are dozens of variations on the theme of initiation but that given by Evan John Jones of the initiate carrying a lighted candle (symbolising past life) into the circle is beautiful in its simplicity compared with other elaborate ceremonies; this candle is extinguished and a fresh light given to the newly affirmed Witch, representing the beginning of life under the protection of the Goddess.

Cole's initiation was even less formal: "I initiated myself. It was my favourite time of the year and my favourite festival. I performed a ritual to give myself the protection of a psychic space, free from daily and mundane atmosphere. Using essential oils to anoint myself and consecrating my magical tools for the first time, I solemnly offered myself, my skills, my abilities to the Lady and the Lord. There were no bonds, whips, threats, black candles or weirdo dramas. Just me, my partner, a few white Co-op candles, some joss sticks, our magical tools (knife, wand, chalice, plate) and a great atmosphere. I was, for those who care to know - naked. Not for the sexual buzz but because when you're naked you're 'warts and all'. No fine clothes to hide inside and 'front' the self you know is false. When you are naked, you are there, seen for what you are. (These days I rarely work naked in the winter, it is too expensive to maintain the heating.)"

Dr Robbins commented on the widely held belief of indiscriminate fornication during the sabbats, in that 'the preoccupation of celibate priests with the niceties of intercourse was insatiable ...' Mike considers it important that outsiders understand that the point of practising 'sex magic' (ie. the rising of sexual energy to be diverted to magical purposes) has to be separated from the Great Rite and/or the erotic symbolism of Witchcraft as a remnant of the old Pagan religion. In his experience modern Wiccan meetings have never been used as an excuse for group sex.

Charges that Witchcraft and Paganism are corrupting or immoral are hotly denied by practising Witches. Cole added: "Most Witches I know are Earth Pagan or Solitary Witches. Sure I've heard the rumours, the gossip of the Pagan scene but that makes nothing but noise. However, those in the Craft who seek publicity, sell books and give sordid interviews with tacky magazines, while describing some fantasied sexual act, repel me ... If Witches who profess respect for The Great Rite profane the act, then they are not Pagans but dealers in selling the sacred."

It is the ceremony of The Great Rite that has been the most frequently misquoted, misrepresented and misused in the eyes of the 'experts'. Often mistakenly believed to be the fictional black mass it is, according to one Witch, probably one of the least performed ceremonies, some covens having never performed it other than symbolically. Another offered the explanation that in its ancient aspect it was performed between two carefully chosen people, in order to produce a magical child, or one blessed with special attributes. The Rite needs only be performed in token and in private but for those who still believe in the erotic aspect, throughout the act the couple need to lie perfectly still, so as not to excite each other, as it is necessary to come to the end of a long invocation before orgasm is reached.

The Great Rite has been repeatedly confused with the black mass and the Mass of Saint Secaire, and by the time all three have been fused together, the true symbolism and meaning behind The Rite is entirely lost - even if it was ever fully understood in the first place. It is therefore important that this myth be exploded once and for all by those in a position to explain the true religious significance of the act.

Under those circumstances it was rather surprising that several of those who offered to help with the research, refused to co-operate by claiming that their oath forbade any discussion of the subject. What made the refusals even more unbelievable was the fact that during a well-publicised case of a Pagan family being wrongly suspected of child-abuse, the police had shown a considerable amount of interest in the activities surrounding The Great Rite. Even this could not persuade them to offer some explanation or clarification, thereby fostering the suspicion that there must be some sinister connotation if they refused to given even the vaguest outline of the religious significance.

Mike however, *was* willing to explain that when The Great Rite is performed, it is normally between a couple who are already in a steady relationship (whether married or not) and is always conducted in private. If this is not the case, it is done symbolically, ie. without the physical sexual act and substituting the symbolism of the athame (the Witches' black handled knife) plunged into the chalice. As part of the religious ceremony, the Great Rite invokes the 'passing of the power' and the assumption of the god-forms, whereby the priest and priestess who are participating become channels for the spiritual energy personified in the archetypal forms of the God and Goddess. Mike concluded by saying: "Again we are dealing with the symbolism and practices which outsiders will find difficult to understand and/or accept, as it is a religious worship totally outside the normal experience of most people in western society."

Paul Greenslade of The Pagan Federation confirms much of Mike's explanation in that The Great Rite is one of the terms bandied around by many and understood by the few. "Explanations are fine" he says "but nothing can really explain the beauty and majesty of what is taking place. In its lowest form it can be seen as an act of ritual sex, and those with small smutty minds will throw up their hands in pseudo shock and cry obscenity. But in the greater reality, it is the union with the divine forces on a metaphysical level, the God and Goddess. It is usual for this to take place with a couple who have been together for some time. If on the other hand, a person is receiving their third degree and they are not in a relationship, it is usual for The Great Rite to be performed in token, ie. by the use of symbolism with the athame and chalice. However, this must be between the initiator and the one being initiated."

In Chris Bray's view the initiation ritual, when properly structured, understood and applied, is a very powerful psycho-dramatic aid, which conveys things intuitively which cannot be learned intellectually. It is true that much of the Gardnerian ritual is reconstructed and that scourging is extraneous; but the initiation ritual itself contains personal insights which cannot be conveyed by logic or intellectual observation. He also feels that the same observations apply to the Third-degree rite, being sick and tired of neo-Pagans who bring their sexual repressions to the Circle:

"There is nothing wrong with healthy HOLY sex; it is the the liberation of suppressed NORMAL sexuality which hallmarks all the Nature religions above paternalistic theocracies. Obviously there will be arrangements for privacy; obviously there will be arrangements for relationships but to miss out this most important act of magic when the Priest and Priestess are actually inflamed by their God and Goddess for the most holy act of sex, is to miss out on the foundation stone of Nature Religion. Over-moralising of this kind is a death-knell to life-loving expression. Are we to create a mock-Christianity where sex magic is barred to all but 'properly married' couples? No double standards here, let us hope."

Almost by tradition, accusations of drug abuse have frequently been hurled at coven members but what is the reaction to those who allegedly mix magic and drugs? "More haste, less speed, seems to be what Witches who use drugs to charge off across the astral, need to bear in mind" is Cole's viewpoint. "Without launching into a great essay about the perils of drugs on the physical self, the perils in terms of ego, illusions, false concepts of ability and the psychic downfall that follows are enough. The word 'witch' means 'wise', so how could anyone who mixes drugs and magic really have the right to be called wise?"

Mike on the other hand presented a more far reaching and objective view: "Again we are entering a controversial area where misunderstandings are rife and cannot be easily solved. The use of natural psychedelics has been known in the Craft but this is a dangerous area where the inexperienced can run into trouble. There are safer methods of attaining psychic awareness and altered states of consciousness, and I would not recommend the use of any form of drug. Having said that, the sacred use of natural psychedelics has to be clearly separated from the abuse of illegal drugs for social reasons. The vast majority of Wicca groups do not use narcotic substances."

The media also relish stories related by satanic survivors of the gruesome and grisly repercussions against anyone trying to break away from the group. Paul Greenslade responded that such stories are generated and foisted upon Pagans by the fundamentalists and the term 'occult' or 'satanic survivor' mostly cover those who, in fundamentalist terminology, have managed to break away from satanic/Witchcraft groups amidst death threats, curses, etc. What we should not loose sight of is the fact that for a very long period of history, belonging to a coven meant death if members suffered betrayal by one of their own. The only way to guarantee the security of the group was to call down terrible penalties on the head of any potential deserter and the traditional oath became part of modern ritual. An almost identical oath is taken by Freemasons today, which has also evolved from the time when secrecy was essential to the safety of the group.

As for leaving a genuine group, Paul doubts whether many people do leave; if they do, however, it is usually with the blessing of other people in the coven. He adds that no one is going to be coerced into staying against their will, as this would be counter productive. Most groups whether they are Pagan or Wiccan, are fairly close knit and harmonious. They need to be, especially if they work a lot together and if a group of several individuals work together over a period of time, they will generate a kind of group-mind. This group mind will only work if there is harmony and respect amongst all those involved. If one person is out of harmony or resents what is taking place, it becomes very difficult for the rest to actually get on and do anything. "So therefore, if someone wishes to leave, nobody with half a brain is really going to make it awkward for them" he added.

Cole's view carried a far more personal note: "Since the only person I work magic with is also my partner, my friend and my wife, if she ceased to wish to be a Witch I would be sad, since it would put a great divide between us. What is the point of forcing a person to do something against their will?"

The satanic survivors' accounts have added to the considerable amount of suspicion surrounding the Craft with tales of ritualised sex, drug taking and child abuse; with all the 'survivors' freely admitting to taking part in devil worship. However, taking Jeffrey Richards' account of how satanic propaganda can infiltrate public self-conscious, we can see how the 'satanic child abuse' scare was allowed to develop to such a degree that in the late 1980s and early 1990s it became a totally fraudulent, but nevertheless terrifying, public scandal. Because of the lack of factual information, the public were willing to accept such survivors' revelations as genuine, especially when they were endorsed by statements from registered charities, social services, politicians and clergy.

The Inquisitors had terrified medieval man with the horror of emasculation at the hands of Witches, but as 20th century woman had already carried out this threat on their behalf, the scaremongerers were obviously channelling their attention to the modern defender of the hearth - the mother. She was constantly being told that her own children were under threat from perverted followers of Satan who lurked around every corner. These seemingly ordinary and respectable women were utilised as unguided missiles to be launched against occultists to break up occult fayres, disrupt spiritualist meetings, attack local Witches in supermarkets and prevent customers from entering occult shops.

It is important to realise that many of these ladies were NOT religious fanatics, but were merely instrumental in carrying the anti-occult campaign out into the street, to further the aims and objectives of fundamentalist organisations. Indiscriminate sex might gain disapproval but the emotive subject of child-abuse, which had already been receiving a considerable amount of press coverage was easily believed to be linked to Witchcraft and Satanism. These accusations triggered off a chain reaction that was potential dynamite, and became even more so as the media took up the stance of Inquisitor.

Chapter 7: Witchcraft and Magic:

uring the months following the alleged ritual abuse disclosures, and despite the numerous letters explaining the origins of the Craft, no one was interested in details of an ancient fertility cult brought out into the light by Dr Margaret Murray in the early 1920s. In her book *The Witch-Cult in Western Europe,* Dr Murray advanced her theory that Witches had merely preserved the old Pagan religion of pre-Christian Europe, which was practised by many classes of the community but chiefly by the more ignorant or those in the less thickly inhabited parts of the country. The book caused a sensation amongst academics and historians, and for the next forty years, the *Encyclopaedia Britannica's* section on Witchcraft quoted her theories as proven fact.

In *The God of the Witches* published in 1933 she enlarged on her theory that the Craft was no more than a native fertility religion with shamanistic overtones, although she personally had no belief in the supernatural or its hidden powers. Her third volume, however, reversed the scholarly acclaim and Dr Murray's theories were dismissed as the senile wanderings of a 90-year old crank. *The Divine King in England* (1954) expounded some of Frazer's *Golden Bough* legends of the sacrificial god, by serving up an impressive list of royal and substitute victims of ritual sacrifice throughout the ages; managing to suggest that nearly every infamous murder in English history could be laid at the door of the Witch-cult!

Also in 1954 she penned an approving introduction to Gerald Gardner's, then controversial, *Witchcraft Today.* Gardner had identified his own modern cult of Wicca with Margaret Murray's ancient fertility religion and she apparently agreed with him. It is understandable that at this point, historians felt she could no longer be taken seriously as a scholar. By contrast, at the same time, anthropologist, E. E. Evans-Pritchard wrote what was to be accepted as a classical source of reference on the enthnography of Witchcraft and similar belief systems following his studies of the African Azande tribe. His usage of 'sorcery' and 'witchcraft' became standard anthropological terms for identifying the use of magic within society and his studies were transposed by his contemporaries as a yardstick for measuring European Witchcraft; thereby placing an extremely effective academic nail in the coffin of the Old Religion and declaring it detrimental to the interests of the community!

Dr Murray's theories, however, weren't so far off beam, if not strictly accurate and it should be borne in mind that in 1921 when her first book was published, that the repeal of the Witchcraft Act was still 30 years away. The term 'pagan' is Roman in origin and derives from "belonging to a village ... long after (the Christian Church) had been established in towns, idolatrous practices continued to be observed in rural districts, so pagan and villager came to mean the same thing." (Brewer's *Dictionary of Phrases & Fable*). Dr Murray maintained that in those isolated communities Witchcraft HAD survived, although she mistakenly dismissed the idea of any mystical or magical power attached to the religion. But equally wrong were her critics, one of whom suggested that ... "her picture of the Witch-cult seems far too sophisticated and articulate for the society with which we are concerned ..."

Chris Bray explained that the magic in Witchcraft is shamanistic in origin and relies upon a knowledge of supernatural properties of things animate and inanimate, 'linked to a courageous and sacred experimentation with Self'. Witchcraft is a life-loving religion linked to an ecological view of the planet which it holds as being sacred and revers the dignity of all things. The Pagan image of the Goddess and the God have frequently been represented as idolatrous but these merely reflect the highest aspirations of each Witch, in reflecting a perfect human quality that they seek within themselves - in the same way that Catholics and Buddhists would possess an image of a saint or the Buddha.

It is also important to stress that Witches do not parody Christian ritual in any part of their ceremonies. In the traditional sharing of wine and cakes which is an integral part of any Witch gathering, the Craft has been accused of parodying the acceptance of the body and blood of Christ. To coven members, the wine and cakes represent the fruits of the Earth, which they share amongst themselves after the ceremony as their ancestors had done hundreds of years before Christianity arrived in these Islands. Evan John Jones suggests that in its most primitive form, the ritual was the physical partaking of the body of the sacrificed Divine King. Neither do Witches use the sign of a cross as a blasphemy; the magic cross is the equal armed cross, representing the four elements and the four cardinal points.

The most famous magical symbol used by all occultists is, of course, the pentagram, the star with five points which symbolises the four elements and spirit. Drawn with one of its five points projecting upwards, it is the symbol of the dominance of the divine spirit over matter, and according to Dion Fortune, a reversed pentagram with the two points projecting upwards, attracts sinister forces because it overturns the proper order of things and demonstrates the triumph of matter over spirit. The pentagram is to the Craft what the cross and crescent are to Islam and Christianity - a mystical symbol and NOT a badge of evil.

In his book introducing Hereditary/Traditional Witchcraft, Evan John Jones describes the natural worship of the Triple Goddess (as maiden, mother and crone - symbolised by the waxing and waning of the moon) and her consort The Horned God (in his dual aspects as the Green Man and the Dark Lord of the Wild Hunt - representing the deity of fertility and death). However, to refer to the Old Religion as merely a throwback to an ancient fertility cult totally avoids the mystical importance surrounding the belief, for this was *never* a simple rustic faith of peasants. The faithful worshipped all aspects of Nature, whether beautiful, bountiful or bloodstained; following the cycles of the seasons in the observation of birth, death and rebirth as represented by the turning of the year.

According to Jones, of equal importance was the recognition of the darker, more mystical side of life, receptive to hidden psychic forces and "the ability to understand that, behind the veil between the known and the unknown worlds of the natural and supernatural, there are powers which were once the birthright of humanity ..." It was this dark side that also required the sacrifice of the Divine King in order that his followers might survive having eaten of his flesh; and the

God-King sacrificing his own life so that his people may live is a recurring theme amongst ancient civilisations.

This mystical or mystery aspect of Paganism appears to be one that is assiduously avoided by all but a few of the more traditionally minded. The late Robert Cochrane was highly critical of the development of the modern Craft in an article written as early as 1964 for *Pentagram* ('The Craft Today'); describing it as an attempt by twentieth-century man to deny the responsibilities of the twentieth century. He felt that many Witches had turned their backs upon the reality of the outside world, pursuing a belief system that failed to recognise the needs of modern living, whilst repeating rituals by rote, rather than by understanding. In consequence, he believed that much of it had become 'static and remote from its original purpose, which was to enlighten the follower spiritually'.

Evan John Jones, who was a member of Cochrane's coven, contends that behind the simplicity of it all was a deeper faith that called for a greater understanding than blind acceptance, which ably demonstrates that dedicated Pagans are not expected to accept 'the word' in its fundamental context. Beneath the exterior of a simple Nature worship and cosy sabbat ceremonies, there lies a deeper tradition through which the devotee 'may perceive the beginnings of that ultimate in wisdom, knowledge of themselves and of their motives'.

In a further article for *Pentagram* ('The Faith of the Wise'), Cochrane attacked the limited perception of the various 'authorities' on Witchcraft: "It is one of the oldest of religions," he wrote, "and also one of the most potent, bringing as it does, Man into contact with Gods, and Man into contact with Self. As such the Faith is a way of life different and distinct from any theory promulgated by the authorities or historians ... It has, in common with all great religions, an inner experience that is greater than the exterior world. It is a discipline that creates from the world an enriched inward vision. It can and does embrace the totality of human experience from birth to death, then beyond. It creates within the human spirit a light that brightens all darkness, and which can never again be extinguished. It is never fully forgotten and never fully remembered."

Unfortunately, Robert Cochrane died as a result of suicide in 1966 and it is generally felt that, although controversial, outspoken, and virtually unknown outside the Hereditary Craft, he could have been an important influence on breaching the divide between the different factions - despite his sarcastic comments about modern Wicca, which caused considerable offence amongst the Gardnerians. Of Cochrane, Doreen Valiente wrote: "There is one thing I know for certain, Robert Cochrane 'had something'. Call it magical power, charisma or what you will. He may have been devious; but he was no charlatan." Although very little information on his beliefs and workings remain available to serious researchers, it is Cochrane's flesh and blood interpretation of Craft doctrine that inspires more credibility than the milk and water variety offered by many other Pagan viewpoints.

Part of that 'totality of human experience' is the acceptance of reincarnation, an intrinsic part of Craft lore, which Evan John Jones described as the soul of the small part of the Godhead returning to its place of origin and re-absorbed into the divine spiritual mass of the Body of God. While the physical body of the present existence is limited to one life span, the soul or the spirit that is the immortal essence of each person survives death, only to be reborn again. And with each rebirth, it is necessary to fulfil the fate that is predetermined by the previous existence.

The most important tenet of *The Pagan Credo* (see Appendix I) on which all Witch-lore is based is: *"An it harm none, do what thou will"*. A simple ethic that governs all Pagan philosophy and thinking. Despite the wider implications of a continuous development of spiritual awareness, the Pagan faith is fundamentally linked with a love of, and a kinship with Nature. The Pagan acceptance of reincarnation strengthens this attitude insofar that they see the Earth as a permanent home, not a temporary stopping-off place. It also emphasises the importance of not consciously committing harm to any living creature. Any obligation to set matters right can only be undertaken by oneself and not avoided by a bodily death.

When Patricia Crowther, a respected figure in the Craft and author, was first initiated in 1960 the only Pagan community was a small number of hereditary Witches in a handful of independent and secretive covensteads dotted throughout the UK. As Paganism began to grow more popular, everyone wanted to join a coven because it appeared to be the only way in which to worship the God and the Goddess. She pointed out, however, that not everyone is suitable or has developed sufficient understanding to take initiation and therefore many remain outside the coven and refer to themselves as Pagans. As the vast majority of Christians do not become priests, so the majority of the 150,000 strong Pagan community do not wish to become Witches.

Pagans perform their ceremonies throughout the year, mirroring the changing seasons with the natural cycles and psychic currents of the planet. These are celebrated at the four Great Sabbats at Imbolc (2nd February); Beltane or May Eve (30th April); Luguasad (1st August) and Samhain (31st October). Between them fall the Lesser Sabbats of the spring and autumn equinoxes and the summer and winter solstices. Of these, Midsummer Eve (21st June) was a popular ancient festival and the Midwinter solstice, better known as Yule (21st December), is still celebrated as Christmas.

This latter festival came under heavy censure from the early Church but it was too deeply entrenched to be abolished and has survived with many of its Pagan elements virtually intact. (According to *Man, Myth & Magic* it was **not until the 4th century that the 25th December was officially declared to be the birthday of Christ** and another 500 years lapsed before it was actually called Christmas.) The date of Easter still depends upon the first full moon after the spring equinox and this festival was also of Pagan origin, being derived from the Scandinavian Goddess, Eostre. Esbats are the monthly, less formal gatherings when coven or group business is attended to and new members initiated.

With the exception of Samhain (or Halloween) all the festivals are lighthearted and those meeting together do so in an act of worship, rather than to perform a magical rite. Samhain marks the end of the year and the commencement of winter, when the veil between the other world and this is lifted; it is a time for remembering and communicating with departed loved ones and by token is a more sombre ritual than the other sabbats. The ancient Britons' observance of communicating with the dead was a well established part of the Old Religion long before the arrival of the Celts. In *The Realm of Ghosts*, Eric Maple comments that with all the ancient tombs, burial mounds, barrows and stone circles, the British Isles must have appeared as a great necropolis to later invaders. Britain is purported to have more ghosts to the square mile than any other country in the world, which suggests a possible regression to our ancestral familiarity with the Underworld in the British love of ghost stories.

This Underworld, however, was not presided over by any Devil and it is important to understand that Satan, Lucifer or the Devil in any guise plays no part in the pantheon of Paganism. The Horned God of the Witches (sometimes called Cernunnos) can trace his origins back to prehistory, as is depicted in cave paintings of the late Stone Age, *predating the existence of the Christian Devil by some 99% of man's life on Earth* - all other periods down to the present occupying the remaining 1%. Witches believe that everyone is responsible for their own actions and regard 'evil' as an imbalance to be corrected, not an independent force or entity.

Of course it is claimed that Paganism by qualification is anti-Christian but again this belief evolves from a basic lack of understanding of the Old Religion. In company with Muslims and Buddhists, Pagans do not accept Jesus as the Son of God - but they *do* recognise him as a mystic, a healer and a teacher of Divine Wisdom. Pagans are taught to be tolerant of all other religious belief systems and regard all sincere religions as different paths to the same truth. Similarly, all holy sites are considered sacred and for that reason, no true Witch would lift a hand in destruction against a church, temple or graveyard of any denomination.

What IS incomprehensible to most Pagans is the Christian ability to reconcile the teaching of humility and compassion with the bloody-minded bigotry that justifies the elimination of any other faith that their Church deems 'false'. Throughout its European history the Church has effectively silenced any opposition by attack or extermination - the Waldenses, Cathars, Templars, Jews, Witches, Druids and the Freemasons - none of whom were devil-worshippers. This war of repression claimed the lives of some estimated 13 million men, woman and children during the Witch-trials alone. Modern Pagans can only view the current persecution as a throw-back to medieval intolerance - and fear the worst.

So what do people discover in Paganism that the orthodox religions cannot offer? Paul Greenslade of The Pagan Federation holds the view that it encourages people to become responsible for their own lives, to be able to think for themselves. He believes that many are attracted because they relate to the worship of the Goddess and the God as a balanced pair; also because it is a religion of love and joy, of sharing, and of seeing good in others as opposed to looking for evil under every stone. Paganism is a living religion that addresses the needs of today - it is not fixed by an ancient revelation that stops it from looking forward to tomorrow. He also suggests that it is because it accepts magic and psychic awareness as being something that everyone possesses to a greater or lesser degree.

Cole was attracted by the reconciliation of opposites; the fact that neither male or female oppressed the other and and holds firmly to the core of his belief which is to HARM NONE. "I am not like the person next door, that is true" he says, "but I am not repeating Christian prayers backwards and mocking their faith. I am not letting blood - I am a vegetarian after all and have been for eleven years or more. As for black candles and up-side-down crosses, long daggers and cockerels - well forget it. I don't abuse children and I live in fear of perverts (who may well be calling themselves Christian, Buddhist, Muslim or Hindu), who try to abduct MY children. It is part of my religion to be tolerant of other faiths and I never try to convert another person to my belief. I don't go in for orgies; I've been happily married for over ten years and I don't frighten or harm people."

Evan John Jones offers a blunt explanation of why many object to the doctrine of the orthodox systems in that as civilisation developed, spiritual advancement was overpowered by material longing. Subsequently, as religion extended its power over the community and, instead of remaining spiritually the servants of humanity, the priesthood elevated itself to the position of master. God could only be approached through an intermediary; his blessing could be withheld or granted by the priest; while default put the offender's mortal soul in jeopardy.

Today's Pagans are not bound by such archaic dogma. They accept that they are responsible for their own destiny, knowing there is no one else on whom blame can be placed. They acknowledge that the penalties incurred in this life must be repaid in the next. Their faith is not one of blind acceptance but one which encourages them to question, explore and demand answers. Their Godhead is neither matriarchal nor patriarchal, but an embodiment of both, to whom they can supplicate direct without fear. They do not need to join in worship with a congregation to be seen to be a believer and can observe their religion in the privacy of their own home, in a wooded glade or on a mountain top if they so desire. They are spiritually attuned to Nature and the Universe and accept that *all* spiritual paths lead to the same ultimate goal. On the whole, the Pagan community appears to have developed an intensely powerful spiritual consciousness which is rare, even amongst today's more orthodox religions.

However, despite the cohesive elements of Paganism there is a sharp divide between those who follow the Mystery Path and those who are content to remain outside the Craft, which is not of recent origin. Robert Cochrane pointed out in 'The Craft Today' that during the persecutions the adherents of the Mystery system went underground and joined forces with the aboriginal beliefs of the mass, and so became part of tradition Witchcraft; centuries passed and the meaning behind much of the ritual was forgotten, or relegated to a superstitious observance to elemental Nature.

These sentiments were echoed by occult author Michael Howard in that it is necessary to accept that the Old Ways were fragmented by the persecutions and often only debased remnants survived in the guise of folklore, seasonal customs and rural superstitions. In the absence of written records, he feels that the task of restoration of the original beliefs has been rendered almost impossible and is comparable to trying to fit together a jigsaw when many of its major pieces are missing or damaged.

In an introduction to the Hereditary Craft in *The Cauldron* he also pointed out that the medievel Witch-cult was more male orientated in some of its forms, the magister taking a more prominent role than the high priest does in contemporary Wicca. "There was also equal and sometimes exclusive worship of the Witch-God which can still be found in many traditional pre-revivalist groups. To a certain extent our perceptions of the historical Craft have been coloured by neo-Pagan and Wiccan ideas which are recent innovations and sadly these have become so dogmatic that any attempt to question their validity is treated as a heretical act of the worst type" ... and goes against the grain of modern neo-Pagan and feminist ideals.

Many sincere and dedicated Pagans prefer to distance themselves from coven practice and, like Nicola, believe that their way represents a belief more in tune with the developing Pagan community than the more Craft orientated/occult/esoteric brigade; defining her approach to the Goddess or Earth Mother as being more Pagan/earthy/ *exoteric*. Whatever their differences; whether their implementing of natural forces is restricted to the use of herbal medicines within the home or engaged in the search for ultimate knowledge, the majority of Pagans are influenced by magic.

Black & White Magic:

Before examining the differences between black and white magic, it is worth mentioning that aspect of the Craft so relished in Witch-trials: a Witch's ability to fly. It is possible that some of the women questioned actually believed that they had taken to the air but the answer to this intriguing mystery probably lies in the ingredients blended into the 'flying ointment' that Witches rubbed into their skins before attending the sabbat.

It has long been suspected that the herbs used in the recipe produced hallucinatory affects, much the same as modern drugs will do. When rubbed onto the skin, the natural properties contained in the ointment could produce the most alarming affects and since no medieval woman would be free from vermin, the preparation coming into contact with flea bites, etc. could cause her to hallucinate dramatically. Aconite, belladonna, water hemlock, and poppy all contain certain toxic substances and all appear regularly in ancient formulae. It has also been suggested that any fats or oils included in the brew, were used to keep out the cold.

However, since Inquisitional confessions were ALWAYS extracted under torture and the Inquisitor ALWAYS put self-incriminating words into the victim's mouth, they have no reliability whatsoever, as hardly any of the innocents who were executed were involved in Witchcraft. Witches have indeed historically used the power of plants for changing consciousness into magical realms, but they certainly knew more than their Inquisitors.

The recipe given by Inquisitional sources is nearly complete in that fats do have a special property for transferring active principles from drugs through the skin (whether broken or not) but that could be ANY fat; not the fat of unbaptised babies as is claimed in Inquisitional propaganda. Chris Bray suggests that this is a chicken and egg situation, insofar as did the Inquisition discover practitioners with a real knowledge of toxic plants, or did they simply hang it onto their victims? "The latter is by far the best bet." he concluded.

Most of the magic worked within the coven is concentrated on psychic and herbal healing and the widest misconception relating to Witch-magic is the casual use of the terms 'black' and 'white' magic. Commonly used to differentiate between beneficial and harmful spell casting, the majority of Witches appearing in the media are anxious to refer to themselves as 'white Witches' and that in itself questions the authenticity of their claims.

Magic *per se* is neither black nor white, good nor evil and it is extremely difficult to define what is meant by magic, as the word has different meanings for different people. To some it merely refers to the cabaret act of card tricks and illusion; others think of it in terms of ignorant superstition; many connect it with a fictional world of wicked Witches and wizards of fairy tale. To many more, the definition falls between a sinister connection with black masses and evil on one hand, and love potions and healing on the other.

In the lead paragraph to the section on white magic in *Man, Myth & Magic*, Eric Maple writes: "White magic can best be described as an 'ancestral science' and that it is in practice, a human technique designed to control the environment. Based on the belief that the forces of Nature can be recruited to serve man's interests, the control of such forces was one of the most important functions of the Pagan priesthood, and it is only comparatively recently (in historical terms) that magic has become divorced from religion."

The age old conflict between the opposing forces of good and evil may only have been the product of over active imagination but it has always attracted the attentions of highly accomplished personalities who are acknowledged as having access to mystical powers. Despite the protestations of exponents of white magic that their esoteric operations were used chiefly for the benefit of their neighbours, the Church remained unsympathetic, refusing to recognise that (as with all scientific principles) magic has its positive and negative aspects. Similarly, practitioners of magic pursue different objectives: some seek power in order to dominate others, whilst others are genuine seekers of wisdom and enlightenment.

Maple also pointed out that what is not generally realised is that in its heyday, before it was outlawed as an evil practice, white magic involved a wide variety of socially useful activities which are not today readily associated with occultism. The rural practitioner was also doctor, veterinary surgeon and detective; called in to cure illness, disease and locate missing belongings. The latter not that far removed from those of Catholic persuasion praying to St. Anthony for assistance in finding lost property!

But even this is an over simplification as we can see from the section on black magic in *Man, Myth & Magic* where the definition is taken one step further: "The distinction between black and white magic is simple in theory: a black magician works for evil ends and a white magician for good. But in practice the distinction isfrequently blurred. For one thing, it rests in the eyes of the beholder and very often white magic is what you work and black magic is what other people work. For another, a man who believes he had magical powers is likely, being human, to use them sometimes to help and sometimes to harm. ... Similarly, modern Witches and Magicians will usually admit their readiness to turn their powers against rival occultists who attack them.

"For Magicians themselves, magic is morally neutral. It works automatically, like a tap. If you turn the taps on in the bath, you get water. You may be filling the bath to wash the baby or to drown him, but your motives do not affect the water supply. ... The authors of the grimoires (or magical textbooks) inherited an old magical tradition that the power of a god can be captured and 'turned on' like a tap, regardless of the Magician's motives. They also inherited a deeper tradition still, that the true goal of the Magician is to find and identify himself with an ultimate unity, underlying and pervading all things. All things are grist to the Magician's mill and all experiences are necessary to him. He must experience and master hatred as well as love, cruelty as well as mercy, evil as well as good. This is the path of the 'Magus' and it is the Magus perverted who makes the master black Magician."

According to Dion Fortune's assessment in the *Qabalah*, the world of magic is on a lower level than the world of intellect and imagination, or the vital, creative forces of Nature. She explained that certain people posses natural magical faculties but unless these are subservient to intellect and imagination, they will tend to be used in the service of negative emotion, resulting in character degeneration.

The real difference then, between black and white magic appears to be a question of *personal* morality and/or intellect, and each person has his or her own moral standard by which they live. A man might commit adultery but could never consider the prospect of beating his wife. To another, beating his wife and children for some real or imagined misdemeanour would be keeping his own house in order, but the prospect of committing adultery with his neighbour's wife would be sinful. To a third party, both practices would be distasteful. It's all a question of values to the individual involved.

Witches, however, do believe that there is an infallible system against the misuse of magical power and that is **The Law of Threefold Return.** It is generally accepted that the dangers in the practice of any form of magic by someone with limited self-control and understanding can cause magic to backfire, especially when the object of the spell is stronger than the one who cast it. Those adept at controlling their magical skills believe that magic involves the power over good AND evil; that there can be no white magic without black. The Magus who cannot destroy cannot create, and in order to use his power benignly, he must first become master of himself. Therefore, the real object of the Magician's art is knowing and controlling himself: the beneficial or harmful effects of his magic are immaterial.

On the subject of Witch-magic Paul Greenslade of The Pagan Federation responded: "Here's a wonderful subject and something that could take up an entire book all by itself. Witches do not go around putting curses on people, this is a legacy from the time when Pagans were being persecuted by the Christians. There is a Craft law which says - "An it harm none, do what you will." This might sound quite easy, or an excuse for doing whatever you feel like, but in reality, it isn't. It means that whenever you are going to do something, such as a love spell, you have to consider in depth just what is likely to take place. If it is going against one person's free will, or nature, then this would be wrong ... If we had half the magic that we are accused of, then we would never have had the persecutions. A lot of the magic that takes place is on the individual - a personal inner transformation, an inner healing that makes us whole."

Cole and Rae are Solitary Witches from Wiltshire; this means that they do not belong to a coven but observe their religion privately at home. According to Cole, most curses are laid by people who are not Witches but who are in highly charged emotional situations and have no idea just how effective a willed or wished negative happening can be when it is flung with emotional charge. To learn how to heal is to learn how to hurt. He also explained that to learn how to work creative healing also requires the knowledge of how to be destructive

- to understand exactly what you are doing and what lore governs each individual act. "The Threefold Law of Return holds true" he says, "If a hex settles, works and causes harm, when it is done it comes home to the sender and threefold in its strength. A lot of people might be a lot happier if they knew this and did not wish ill on others."

Professor Jeffrey Richards cites Norman Cohn's research demonstrating how the Church managed to create a "new and wholly artificial construct out of four previously separate and distinct elements: folklore, Witchcraft, ritual magic and Devil-worship."

This new formula effectively concealed the true distinction between high and low magic, ie. that used for good or evil ends. Cohn opined that medieval Witchcraft was essentially low magic focusing on the folk medicine of the local wise woman who was skilled in herbal healing and midwifery. This was largely confined to the lower classes in the community and practised by individuals rather than groups. High magic was considered to be a science, practised by learned men involving formal rituals, books of magic lore (grimoires) and the conjuring up of demons. His most important point was that *the Magi invoked God and not the Devil*, and that the demons summoned were servants to do the magician's bidding, not as masters instructing the Magi in the Devil's work. "Neither form of magic involved the worship of the Devil, orgies, infanticide, or cannibalism." he concluded.

Chris Bray endorsed this view in that ultimately magic is neither black nor white; good nor evil. It is simply *THE CREATIVE FORCE* and that we should be grateful for the fact that aspiring magicians have to study long and hard to gain any proficiency in its use - which in itself brings a responsibility and wisdom, and invariably protects against its misuse. He was also quick to point out that being a Pagan doesn't necessarily make an individual superior, nor does it make them infallible or even wise - as he was later to find out to his cost.

Chapter 8:   From Inside the Circle:

hen the ideas for the *Malleus Satani* were first discussed with Chris Bray, he expressed a concern that it would be difficult to give a broad analysis of modern Witchcraft due to the fact that if 100 different Witches were interviewed, the results would show 100 different ways of approaching their chosen Path. This point is ably demonstrated, not so much by the different ways of approaching the Goddess and God, but by the attitudes that some Pagans show to each other.

Cole, aged 35, and his partner Rae, are our Solitary Witches, whose approach to the Craft is "very environmental, very keyed into Earth and personal healing." For Cole, the non-sexist, non-hierarchial belief system that held the Earth in reverence attracted him to the Craft and Paganism - in addition he fell in love with a Solitary Witch and handfasted (ie. married) with her. "But she never persuaded me, recruited me or requested that I become a Witch. Witches, as you may have noticed, don't go knocking door to door to make conversions, even in one to one relationships."

Many Pagans pursued a line of enquiry through occult books or magazines in the first instance; Rufus came into contact with Wicca by answering an advertisement in the *Spare Rib* publication, later becoming joint editor of the Pagan journal, *The Pipes of Pan*. Nicola discovered the Pagan religion when she read a copy of Janet MacCrickard's booklet, *The Way of the Goddess* which made sense of a lot of things she had been feeling. "It was wonderful" she says "to find other people who felt the way I feel about Earth; who felt deep spiritual connection to the seasons, cycles and changes of Nature."

All this sounds neatly packaged and organised but there is one underlying fact that surfaces quite distinctly in conversations with Pagans - that there appears to be distinct fissures amongst the foundations of Paganism which could bring the whole edifice crashing down. During the spring of 1989 *The Pipes of Pan* published a hard hitting article entitled 'United We Stand - Divided We Fall' which reflected Chris Bray's own experience, in questioning the apathy of fellow-Crafters in responding to the slanders of the anti-occult campaign. Not only did the writer criticise those who backed away from the threat, but delivered a sharp rebuke to those who disparaged the efforts of others who did attempt to defend their faith. The prognosis warned that the occult world, and the Craft in particular, was in danger of going the same way as the Christian Church, into schism and split; pointing out that whatever their differences, the Christian sects were at least united in their opposition to occultism.

Cole added: "Sadly it is true, that like all religions, Paganism has attracted its share of 'people who know best', and who practice little or no tolerance. They might be under the name of neo-Pagan, Wiccans, Hereditary, Solitary, Dianic, Faerie or Celtic Shaman and make loud noises about right, tradition, initiation and so on. But whatever they may be, they are none of them Pagan, if they are not working for the good of the planet; not one one them can claim worship the Goddess if they are not involved with the environmental struggle to save the planet. After all, a Pagan believes that life, all life on the Earth on which we walk, is sacred. Pagans are unified by their love and worship of the Earth Mother and the Green Man, and amongst them there is no gulf of misunderstanding. The misunderstanding lies between those who are Pagan and those who like to think they are."

But Patricia Crowther's reaction to the question of division within the Craft is not as simplistic as Coles's: "The Craft is the Mystery Priesthood WITHIN the Old Religion. It has always been selective of members, which is why a coven is kept to 13 people - or less. Nowadays, we have neo-Pagans and the other groups you mention - so we have a healthy, growing population who worship the Old Gods, and this is how it should be."

On the other hand, Paul Greenslade feels that much of the dissension depends a little on the information source, since some Pagan publications are defiantly anti-Craft. There are those who think they want to become Witches until they discover the amount of work and dedication this takes; who then back away with the excuse that they didn't like the way the coven operated. According to Paul, the majority of people within the Craft just get on with what they are doing: "It's normally those on the outside who are doing all the shouting, and most of those who do the complaining are basing their arguments on what they have read or heard, not on what they know, which is a big difference."

Patricia Crowther continued her explanation: "The only way that the Craft is divided, is that there are so many who start covens without first being initiated. I was taught that the Craft HAS to be inherited. You must be brought in by an already *bona fide* initiated Witch. Down the line, for at least three hundred years, this has been so, and this is how the Mysteries are kept alive and certain things kept from the common people. And this has nothing to do with being 'better than thou'. I was brought in by Gerald Gardner - and his was an hereditary line, as was my other initiator into the Inner Mysteries. It is not fair to those who seek initiation, to pretend to authority, when such is not the case. Fortunately, there are certain things that are never written down. They are communicated orally at an appropriate time."

And it is necessary to understand what is meant by **initiated** Witchcraft, for many books on the Craft often include references to the rank or 'degrees' within the covenstead. Mike explained that when one talks of degrees, the subject is limited to the Gardnerian/Alexandrian forms of Witchcraft. Those reaching the Second and Third Degree are the more experienced members of the coven who may instruct new members. On attaining the Second Degree they may even form their own group, as it is not permissible for a First Degree Witch to become a High Priestess or Priest.

Patricia Crowther confirms that there are three degrees of attainment within the Craft and these have to be worked for, as in any course of study - normally over a period of three to four years.

Cole on the other hand pointed out that within the path of the Solitary Witch there are no degrees that one can pass or fail. There are however, constant trials and difficulties; initiations which each person must meet in their own way as they walk along the path. He suggested that in a sense it might be harder than working within a coven, as a Solitary Witch is alone, with only conscience, integrity and common sense as a guide.

These sentiments are borne out in part by Evan John Jones who stressed in *Witchcraft - A Tradition Renewed*, that the fact that a person is not a member of any coven, or has never been initiated into any coven, should never let it hold them back from worshipping the Old Gods. It means that they have to find their own Path, and he also suggested that it can be harder, but in some ways a more satisfying means of gaining wisdom. The Hereditary Craft does not use the degree system; neophytes being trained for a year and a day before their induction or formal acceptance into the coven, group, tradition or family.

But not all criticism of Craft practice comes from the uninitiated. Rufus openly published his own reservations in *The Pipes of Pan*: "I've been using the term 'simple country Pagan' to describe my spritual path for quite a few years now, but usually folk haven't understood much of what it meant ... The word 'Pagan' was chosen primarily in distinction to the word 'Witch'. It was less commonly and less positively used term then than at present. Frequently it was used by Wiccans in a disparaging way (and still is) to dismiss the uninitiated, those who were interested in the Goddess and the Old Religion but who were "not one of us". I had come to feel a deep dissatisfaction with Wicca as I had experienced it. I don't feel that these experiences were unrepresentative as I had been initiated into three (allegedly) different Traditions and had attained the status of High Priest."

Nicola defines the word 'Pagan' as suggesting different things to different people. "To some," she says, "it simply means 'non-Christian'; to a few, mistakenly linking it with the nonsense of black magic horror films, it is a word to be feared; to an increasing number of people it has a very specific meaning, both in terms of religion and a way of life. I call myself a Pagan," she continues, "one who feels the spiritual connection between myself and all of Life, knowing we are all children of the Goddess. I try to live according to the cycles of Nature and to harm no living thing.

"Paganism is not a dogmatic faith. There are no holy books, prophets or saviours. There is no One True Way - rather a great diversity of approach to the faith, and a great variety of creative ways in which it finds expression, naturally arising from the infinite diversity of life. Some may argue that it is not necessary to be a Pagan in order to live in harmony with Earth. We believe though, that it is not sufficient to care for our planet simply because it is common sense, just to ensure that our species will survive."

However, a letter appearing in the *Lamp of Thoth* magazine expressed anxiety over the colourless, uncompromising image that was being foisted onto the Goddess, in that more and more individuals were using, not a threefold knowing and powerful deity, but a single formed Goddess, dealing solely with the sweeter things in life. "A Victorian image of a woman on a pedestal, devoid of all but beauty, without strength, warmth or wisdom. We are concerned that these people, misinformed or looking for a socially acceptable form, are creating a poor psychological pattern for themselves and an imperfect astral form, unable to fulfil her role as Maiden, Mother and Crone."

Also in the *Lamp of Thoth*, Miriem Clay-Egerton expressed her concern that although "chauvinistic males have ruled the roost for a long time and it is time for a change, does it automatically follow that the Great Mother only must be supreme ... that the God be reduced to the status of a celestial toy-boy, a form of randy, incestuous choir-boy? Surely we are in danger then of female chauvinism?"

A dedicated and committed Pagan, Nicola is joint editor of the magazine *The Pipes of Pan* mentioned above, which also incorporates the newsletter of something very important to her, the Pagan Parenting Network. There are many young Pagan parents who now prefer to educate their children at home and it is interesting to hear some of the answers given in favour of the benefits of undertaking the task themselves. In a letter to the Pagan Parenting Network, one mother stated that she did not want to lose her children to the materialism, cynicism and violence that constantly bombards people in today's society. Ellie prefers not to trust something as precious as her three children's education to the 'system'. In believing that children should be free, another felt that they can suffer from terrible pressures at school which can give rise to learning difficulties.

Founded in 1984, the Pagan Parenting Network, offers a support group for those home educating their children but there appears to be some reluctance among Pagan parents to share their actual beliefs with their children. Nicola suggested that many may have been put off rearing their children as Pagans in the face of current media hype regarding child-abuse; a postscript by Rufus adds that another reason for Pagan parents not involving their children, is that they are not practising Paganism as a religion but rather an adults only occult club. "Of course" he adds "there is the other aspect that parents may not want to run the risk of a small child chatting away to the neighbours to reveal the fact that his parents are Pagans."

No one can deny the values of teaching children from a very young age, a sense of responsibility for the Earth and all its creatures, but education does not stop there. If children are encapsulated in a culture vacuum, then surely they run the risk of becoming as narrow in their subsequent adult thinking as fundamentalist children. The world can be an ugly place but no one can live the life of an aesthetic in this day and age; sooner or later children will be exposed to the contrariness of their fellow humans and, as a result of a differing lifestyle, experience problems in communication. By depriving children of outside stimuli and not allowing them to experience at first hand how others live, parents could also be narrowing the chances of their young being able to meet and mix with those outside their own environment.

Philip responded: "We can actually provide quite a good technical education (not that we are sure it's needed), possibly rather better than most schools and are happy to teach any subject to A-level. Children don't need to decide on their careers at age 5!"

Cole however had a slightly different perspective on the education of his own son. "The path of Witchcraft has less impact on my son than the belief in Paganism. Basically he will not be a Witch until he is eighteen, and only then if he wishes. We have no desire to 'make him a Witch' but Paganism does influence his life: A low consumerist life style and a belief in a Goddess as well as a God".

For eight months Cole and Rae did home educate their son but respected his wishes to return to school. Being alone at home, and seeing that he wished to become a doctor, they considered their abilities as teachers were not good enough. "The school knows he is a Pagan and that we are Witches, and there is no problem. My son attends all the usual assemblies and sings all the songs they sing; he goes to Church and mimes the words to prayers if he doesn't feel like speaking them aloud. He is taught, that like all faiths Pagan to Roman Catholic, there are good and bad people in all religions. No doubt he will want to leave home at eighteen, as my stepdaughter has, and fend for himself in the world.

"There is no point in his being unaware of Christianity; for Jesus was a wise teacher and a holy man, and if his followers did as he taught, there would be less intolerance and less violence in this world. I think it is important that my son isn't held in a 'precious bubble' of Pagan purity. If Paganism is to be accepted by the community in which Pagans live, then they, the Pagans, must integrate and participate, and so must their children."

But whilst those spearheading the counterattack accuse others of 'plastic Paganism', the moderates object to the big boots and boxing gloves approach of those carrying the fight to the very doorsteps of the Establishment. Both sides adamant that theirs is the only way to promote understanding and recognition of their faith. One would assume that with the 'satanic child-abuse' campaign gathering momentum that all Pagan parents would have banded together to defend themselves against such allegations.

This proved not to be the case; some even dismissed Social Services' dawn roundups of children as none of their concern, because the majority of cases did not affect anyone with genuine Pagan involvement. As a result, the opportunity for passing valuable information between readers of occult publications was lost because those in one group were unaware of happenings affecting members of another. Paul Greenslade believes that many Pagans and Wiccans didn't get involved because they thought that whatever happened, it wouldn't affect them. Likewise a lot of Craft people are relatively secretive and their beliefs not generally known, so again they felt that the anti-occult campaign had nothing to do with them.

Several Pagan publications even stated that as far as they were aware, there had been NO cases of Pagans having children taken into care or worse, "because of allegations of 'satanic abuse', nor even of any otherwise unprovoked investigations." This was incorrect - there HAD been cases of Pagan children being taken into care as S.A.F.F files show and several parents lost custody cases because of their Pagan views. In fact, the authorities had successfully gagged parents by lawful process, which prevented any of them from contacting organisations such as the S.A.F.F for help and this is why no details surrounding the cases were made public.

The often-cited case involving a Hull family resulted from malicious allegations made by a neighbour and so-called fellow Pagan. This young family found themselves in the centre of an investigation by Social Services because of some anonymous tip-off through the local N.S.P.C.C. The mother, a High Priestess and a well-known figure at psychic fayres, was visited three times by a social worker and a policewoman, who questioned her about her religious beliefs (particularly The Great Rite), and conducted a search of her home.

Questions of this nature were totally and utterly superfluous in a proper investigation into the welfare of a child but the family were unable to protest because they were terrified that their son would be taken into care. As a result of S.A.F.F intervention the case was dropped and the family completely exonerated, but an even more terrifying aspect of this case shows that ANYONE can ring up the N.S.P.C.C, police, social services or any of the child orientated charities and place a complaint. The mentality and motivations of the source (who is allowed to remain anonymous) is apparently NOT questioned, no matter how badly they defame a character.

There are other cases known to the S.A.F.F including Mark, whose children were taken into care due to the actions of a local group of Christian teachers, who accused him of being involved in 'satanic child-abuse' - because he's a Morris dancer and has New Age interests! And Wendy, whose daughter is in the care of another woman; the same person who accused Wendy of 'satanic child-abuse' and obtained custody of the child, thereby depriving the girl of her natural mother.

Several well known personalities in the Pagan community are aware of other problems within the Pagan movement whereby members are growing away from the true religious commitment to the Old Ways. Rufus expressed a profound dissatisfaction with those whose primary concern is with the working of magic whilst overlooking the religious aspects of Paganism.

"I was not at first interested in the concepts of magic-working and other occult ideas that seemed to go with Wicca. It was a new and challenging area of learning at first but over a period of time it began to feel increasingly alien to me ... My experience has been that many of those describing themselves as Witches see magic-working as the principal focus of their activity, almost to the point of obsession. One could not simply celebrate, say, the turning of the year at Winter Solstice for itself ... without seizing the opportunity for some sort of magic working."

Chris Bray, on the other hand, is concerned that neo-Paganism is becoming so far removed from its roots that in many cases it "has been dogmatised into a completely separate animal, based rather on anthropology and mythology than on its eternal magical perspectives". He feels that the mere fact that any group of Pagans can get away with promoting the religious perspectives WITHOUT an understanding of the magical perspective is testimony to how far its followers have travelled from the true nature of Paganism.

"Other aspects of the occult are similarly castrated" he added. "Ideas like: you can't be a real Pagan unless you are a vegetarian; or homosexuals have no place in a male-female coven; any form of artistry is an expression of the Goddess no matter how indulgent; we would all be better people if we just concerned ourselves with nice things; animals are so sacrosanct that any human found harming them should themselves be harmed. All these absolutes cause a prejudice which overlooks the underlying perceptions and nature of humans. To my mind it is in plumbing the depths of one's psyche and releasing the shackles of Self which is the real work of ALL occult paths."

Returning to the article published in 1964 by Robert Cochrane ('The Craft Today'), which illustrates that even then there were those whose motives were suspect ... "it would appear that the Craft has rapidly become an escape hatch for all those who wish to return to a more simple form of life and escape from the ever-increasing burden of contemporary society. In many cases the Craft has become a funk-hole, in which those who have not been successful in solving various personal problems hide, while the storm of technology, H-bombs, and all the other goodies of civilisation pass by harmlessly overhead."

Cole is equally alarmed by the cavalier attitude some Pagans have towards the faith. "When I look at these folk, I feel frustrated; I no longer wish to share with them the name or label Witch or Pagan. I wish to be something else. They somehow trivialise, belittle, make shallow my religion. That it can be bought with a cheque book, along with that plink plonk musak and occult bric a brac, makes me sick. How come they didn't know they were Pagans and Witches years back - before the fashion? I don't want to give up and draw away from this horrible onslaught. To withdraw from it all for good. It has to pass. I shall just stay clear of it. Observe it. But it does disgust me. As I said before, somewhere between the seedy old shop and the one with the sliced and diced crystals the balance was lost."

Much has been said in the press concerning the immorality of the Craft but Witches correctly attribute the evil acts of man to man himself, as a result of the imbalance and spiritual immaturity within the average person. Much of this imbalance they believe, is caused by the perpetuation of anarchistic religions which teach by example rather than question the inconsistencies of one's own belief, ie. that it is preferable to project one's sins onto others - "The Devil made me do it."

During the research for *Malleus Satani*, the author received several letters from a Born Again Christian who refuted the possibly of man being answerable for his own evil: "One should guard against investing man with more personal responsibility than he can rightly claim as his own." This typical example of fundamentalist cop-out was in response to an article the author had written on the subject of karma and reincarnation. In another part of the letter it was claimed that to affirm that Satan does not exist is to call Christ a liar, therefore the existence of the Devil was a proven fact!

Despite the prejudice and victimisation suffered by fellow Witches, Cole firmly believes that all Pagans should stand up and be counted: "The anti-occult campaign plays on peoples fears and prejudices, touching on the parts of the mind that have no knowledge, no awareness, no information. This part of the general public's mind will remain dark, sordid and infested with lies, until Pagans and Witches have the guts to take their personal courage to the limit and speak out. To use all opportunities both in private and public life, to educate people about themselves."

However, the repercussions of attempting to do so were too frightening for Jan after she went along to her local television station and offered them an interview with a High Priestess in an attempt to alleviate some of the media hype surrounding the Craft. The short interview itself went off well and Jan was well treated by the programme makers. The interview was shown at peak-viewing time and unfortunately her face became known to local fundamentalists; when subsequently attending a local psychic fayre, she was met with cries of "Burn the Witch" from a hostile crowd. Being the mother of two teenage children, Jan decided that discretion was the better part of valour and will not take part in any further attempts to improve the public image of the Craft.

Heather suffered for weeks at the hands of a gang of religious bullies after they found out she was a Witch. She appealed to the police for help after receiving repetitive, anonymous threatening and obscene telephone calls; also demonstrations of up to 20 men chanting abuse and exposing themselves outside her flat, and being treated to parcels of excreta on her doorstep. The police suggested that since they could not offer her protection on a permanent basis, that she should move out of town.

Stuart is an occultist who attracted the attention of a local Pentecostal vicar when he underwent a period of emotional stress during family problems. The cleric persuaded him that all his problems were due to his occult involvement and persuaded him to renounce it and give 'witness' of his sins. Stuart found himself a local personality, used to demonstrate an example of a soul that had been saved. His redemption was recorded in the local press and he found himself being gulled into admitting he was a Satanist - which was a complete fabrication. He had to renounce Satan, burn all his occult books and was even labelled as an attempted suicide - all of which was untrue. These activities attracted the attentions of the national press, who printed the juicy story in all its gory detail. Fortunately, Stuart began to see the church for what it was and broke away from the Pentecostals, returning quite happily to his occult studies.

Michael Howard, however, defends the decision of ordinary Pagans not to come out of the closet despite the fact that such shy behaviour is condemned by those who have already taken the giant leap into the public limelight. "Not everyone makes their living from the occult scene or lives in urban or city areas where religious eccentricity is semi-tolerated as part and parcel of the cosmopolitan social milieu."

Cole and Rae have been fortunate in having understanding teachers at their son's school and a family who regard them as a mixture of interesting and unfortunate. "No one ever asks us directly what we do, or why, but there is a level of tolerance and good humour. The black cat on the broom stick and the cauldron, haven't been mention for years, not since the book came out. Now that is a way of making the relatives feel more mellow about you. Rae wrote a book about how we work magic and worship, and when it came out there was a mixture of pride and encouragement for the next one.

"Since then, I suppose we are thought of as 'arty' and 'alternative', with a dash of spicy 'occult' thrown in for good measure. But whatever faults may lie between me and the best of my relatives, they are nothing to the other relatives, those who would regard me as natural kindling if they knew. But all in all, we are lucky Rae and I. We have families who might not wish to be Pagan but who tolerate our wish to be. I've never discussed my belief with any member of my family but then I hope they think better of me than to believe I would harm anyone or anything."

But under the banner of anti-occultism, even high street traders are not safe from the attentions of the fundamentalists. One local bookdealer was confronted by an irate customer, admonishing him for stocking books on occultism. Now this particular shop only supplies a small selection of very general occult subjects, nothing heavy or outrageous, and on his refusal to desist from selling such material, the customer bought out his entire stock. He merely replied: "Thank you madam" and promptly restocked his shelves. Another second-hand bookdealer was harrassed by a fundamentalist group who insisted he bow to their dictates of what should be sold on his stall; when he refused in no uncertain terms, they moved onto a nearby stall in the market to hand out their anti-occult leaflets. Needless to say, our local occult shop run by an experienced psychic healer, also ran the gauntlet of excessive fundamentalist interference.

As a result of the scurrilous attacks made against its reputation, The Sorcerer's Apprentice in Leeds found itself in the position of having to issue 'A Statement of Intent' to defend its operation. The shop has been established occult centre for over 15 years and during that time has built up a client file of over 40,000 people from all walks of life and all levels of society. The shop stocks over 20,000 books including those on the comparative religions: Buddhism, Shintoism, Islam, Christianity, Hinduism, etc. as well as astrology, divination and alternative forms of healing. None of the books stocked by The Sorcerer's Apprentice incite the reader to break the law or commit any crime.

The owner's philosophy is to provide an access point to ALL forms of human belief and accords adults with the intelligence to decide for themselves what is, or what is not, appropriate. Even though there is no legal statute to enforce them to do so, the proprietors have always applied a voluntary restriction on the sale of goods or books to minors and require parental permission before accepting orders form under 18s. "Not because there is any danger in the occult but to silence ignorant critics" Chris Bray added.

They do however warn customers against the more nefarious and unscrupulous vendors of occult artefacts "You will simply not believe the tricks some of these cowboys get up to," warned Chris. "We know you won't believe it because hundreds of people have been suckered-in to giving these crooks their hard earned cash, which is how they can pay for their ultra-large advertisements and still have cash left over to gloat. Like the 'decorative joss stick burners' which turn out to be lumps of plasticine. The 'full set of magic candles complete with holders' which turn out to be children's birthday cake candles in little plastic holders. The 'purification bath sachets' which are in reality herbal teabags with a spot or two of essential oil. One Witch Queen we know of, bought some salts from Boots and re-packaged it as a 'purification bath', later selling off the pyramid shaped boxes as pyramid kits."

* * *

Public impressions would be wrong in thinking that Christian fundamentalism is aimed solely at occultism/Witchcraft, and the danger such fanatics present to society at large is best described by Kevin from Liverpool, who fell foul of a group of Evangelicals and tells his own story:

"For many years I have been researching different religions and investigating different religious beliefs. That is, Paganism, T.M. Krishna, Christianity, Mormonism and Jehovah Witnesses. Finally I am a member of the Baha'I faith, which is tolerant of all beliefs. *(It also teaches the unity of all religions and the unity of mankind - SR.)*
My awful experience began when I started to attend Evangelical Christian Meetings (where they speak in tongues and generally freak out). After one meeting I was chatting with one of the Elders and expressed a great interest in Paganism and general Old World religions. He looked a bit shocked but didn't really make any

comment. A week later he asked me if he and some of the others could come back to my place after the meeting and get to know me socially.

I drove home with two car loads of people behind me - eight in all. After I let them into my flat, they immediately started speaking in 'tongues' and said that the Devil had possessed me. I started laughing but that just made them worse. They went from room to room, still speaking in tongues, chanting and praying. Two of them put their hands on my head to cleanse me of evil spirits; I began to think that these people were totally off their heads but things got more serious.

They looked at my bookshelves and started taking out books which they thought were not their particular brand of Christianity. All my books on Witchcraft, Gnosticism, Buddhism, etc were removed and I was powerless to stop them as I am disabled. They even took away my philosophy books including Bertrand Russell's, *Why I Am Not A Christian*. (I don't bloody well blame him, I thought.) They took away a brass plaque which had religious symbols on it and also a small black pyramid.

The situation began to get frightening because some of them were becoming rather hysterical but I was more angry than anything else, and I wanted them out of my flat as soon as possible. I asked them where they were taking my books and things but the Elder just said: "They'll be destroyed." The Elder was a nineteen year old (he was in my politics A-level class at college and at that time he was very introverted), and he was loudly demanding the Devil to leave the flat and said he could "sense his evil presence here".

Then they all looked in the garden and noticed the fishpond; I had painted on the flagstones around the pond some runes which spelled "Peace, Love & Harmony", but they thought it was a magic circle. Things got ridiculous as they began walking around the pond, speaking loudly in tongues and shouting "Jesus! Jesus save him!" and trying to scrub out the painted letters with their shoes. When I told them it only said "Peace, Love & Harmony" they didn't believe me and the Elder said he knew a Witches' circle when he saw one! I was really annoyed and embarrassed should any of my neighbours see them.

Finally they left - with a large black bin liner containing my books and religious artefacts They probably stole a total value of about

£200. The whole event probably took about an hour, but it seemed like it was going on for ages. I thought about contacting the police but I didn't bother as I thought this might provoke more hassle from the Evangelicals. What is so frightening is that out of their 80 or so membership, well over half of them are school teachers ... "

What makes this victimisation even more despicable is the fact that Kevin is a thalidomide victim, without arms or legs, and is entirely dependent on others. A spokesman for the S.A.F.F commented: "He should have called the police, not because they could have intervened but because he would have obtained proof other than his own testimony and because if and when the Evangelicals return, he would be in a position to demand police action".

* * *

Mike, however, feels that the basic problem with the public image of the occult in general and the Craft in particular, is that it is in essence totally alien to the average person especially the orthodox church-goer. "This is partly because most people have alienated themselves from their psychic roots and Nature, and partly because of the image which many Witches promote publicly. As stated earlier, there are beliefs and practices which your average person will never understand - and it may not even be feasible to bother to educate them!"

Chapter 9: The Siege of the Sorcerer's Apprentice

It was entirely without warning in the spring of 1988 that The Sorcerer's Apprentice became the focus for a concerted and highly inflammatory, three year campaign to destroy occultism at source. The hysteria-mongers had prepared their infamous dossier with the help of several quisling occultists, who had provided a valuable insight into the occult scene, naming names, magazines, shops and organisations. In reality, this dossier was simply a potted review of U.K organisations, businesses, publications and individuals, but it was used by anti-occult campaigners as 'evidence' of the upsurge in Witchcraft - which they considered to be the same as Satanism.

Chris Bray had already inadvertently drawn attention to himself when he had helped the *BBC Open Space* team put together the occult half of the 'Lucifer over Lancashire' programme, which had been based on claims that unemployed youngsters were turning to the occult. Chris had arranged for *bona fide* representatives to appear and given guidance to the programme makers in order to prove that there was no foundation in the claims.

In April 1988, the anti-occult campaign began in ernest with the the House of Commons outburst, which singled out, named, misrepresented and slandered The Sorcerer's Apprentice and its owner. "... In the city of Leeds can be found the flashmail order centre of The Sorcerer's Apprentice. Just up the hill is the large store called Astonishing Books under the same control. This business is founded on books on Witchcraft, black magic, satanic rituals and other occult practices ... It is common knowledge that Witchcraft initiation rituals involve the abuse of children ... "

In the media follow-up, interviews were given decrying The Sorcerer's Apprentice by saying that shops 'like this' should be closed. Consolidating the opening gambit with a blaze of media hype formulated on just two alleged cases of child sexual gang abuse (neither of which were eventually proven to have any occult connection), claims were also made that 4000 children were being sacrificed each year by Satanists.

At the same time, an official complaint was made to the Leeds police about The Sorcerer's Apprentice's operations but since the staff and owner had an excellent relationship with the police and the local authorities, the attempt to further harass the business failed at the first hurdle.

However, in October 1988, Chris Bray was invited to participate in another radio programme to repudiate the charges being made in an ever increasing number of anti-occult articles and, in a confrontation with one of the journalists responsible, publicly shredded his evidence and made him look foolish. By openly supporting genuine occultists, and in rebuffing the allegations so competently, Chris little realised that he had put himself, his family and his livelihood in the firing line for total victimisation by the powerful anti-occult machine that was waiting in the wings.

These early articles were the precursor of a trail of sensational and despicable publicity based upon the testimony of fanatically religious satanic survivors and paranoid dossiers. Compiled by American and British Christian fundamentalists, the allegations promoted oddball theories of world-domination, secret societies and global crime; linking cases of known psychopaths wherever necessary, all on the flimsiest of pretexts. The campaign lasted five years and successfully tricked not only the British public into believing that satanic/occult ritualised child-abuse existed, but quite a few uninformed occultists too!

Chris Bray has since discovered that the dividing line between gullible fundamentalists and gullible occultists was extremely vague and during the anti-occult campaign, he learned of at least three self-styled, and self-righteous Pagans, who helped the fundamentalist cause by supplying background information and incorrect opinions, thereby supporting the campaign and jeopardising other occultists, whilst safeguarding themselves from attack.

During February 1989, investigative researchers began making overtures to Chris in an attempt to persuade him to take part in an interview for a proposed programme on the occult-linked ritual abuse allegations. He declined the invitation, pointing out that the fanatical theories were sheer fantasy and provided programme researchers with documented evidence to substantiate it; they were also invited to talk about the anti-occult campaign off camera. In the meantime, The Sorcerer's Apprentice had compiled and published *The Occult Census* results as further proof that occultism was not a threat to society. A copy was sent to everyone who had, to date, been involved in the campaign; police, all media contacts, fundamentalists and occultists alike.

Chris Bray's intelligence network had disclosed that the television programme makers were planning a hatchet job on occultism; he also discovered that the researchers were being fed information by certain Christian fundamentalist groups. As information was collated from behind the scenes, Sorcerer's Apprentice reconnaissance revealed that the programme makers had also 'fingered' the business for implication in the programme. In an attempt to pre-empt this, Chris wrote and offered to assist with background information about genuine occultism and the truth behind the anti-occult campaign, but refused to be implicated and declined to be interviewed.

Nevertheless, the programme makers persisted in making numerous repetitive requests for interviews, both by telephone and letter, until Chris was obliged to instruct his solicitor to write and state unequivocally that: "Although Mr Bray was willing to talk to them about genuine occultism and answer any questions off screen to assist with their investigations, he refused point blank to be filmed or recorded."

A few weeks later, during May, the manager of Astonishing Books, spotted two men stationed at a park bench across the road; one of them held a video camera, partly obscured by a blue coat which he was using to conceal the camera. Chris called in the police but since there had been no infringement of the law, nothing could be done. As soon as the police had driven off the television crew openly set up their camera equipment on a full-sized tripod, and began taking pictures through the upstairs windows of The Sorcerer's Apprentice using telephoto lenses. Stationing themselves at the rear, front and side of the building more of the crew arrived and laid siege to the bookshop; photographing all that went on in the shop and through the upstairs office windows. Chris telephoned the police again.

Ten minutes later the same police sergeant returned, together with a community constable. As they walked through the shop door a camera crew ran after them to gain entry. The door was slammed in their faces and locked, whereupon the cameraman began to take shots through the shop windows of what was happening inside the building and stationed themselves outside the door, blocking entry. Chris instructed a member of staff to unhook the shop's security camera and video the television crew's actions which were, in his opinion, now causing a breach of the peace.

He realised that, if the team were willing to behave so badly when the police were present, there was a grave likelihood of fisticuffs after the police had left the scene. Also he couldn't be responsible for the actions of any customers on whom the team might force their attentions, so a breach of the peace was likely. It appeared that television journalists could inflict themselves upon any innocent citizen until they snapped, and THEN the police would simply press charges against both parties involved. Either way, any clue as to the cause of the upset would be edited out and the investigative journalist would have his 'confrontation' finale.

After judging the matter from all sides, in order to protect both his staff and any customers who might be set upon by the television crew, Chris Bray decided to close the shop and have the police escort staff safely out of the building to limit any further harassment or incident. In order to confound the beseigers ever further, he broke out the previous year's Halloween stock and made all his staff wear plastic Dracula masks.

The uproar on the busy main road had drawn a sizeable crowd who now ringed The Sorcerer's Apprentice three-deep, waiting to see the event unfold and no doubt they considered it great fun. They were almost as astonished as the television team when seven Draculas rushed out of the building leaping and dancing with two perplexed and embarrassed policemen bringing up the rear. Chris's car sped forward as the other camera crew dived out of the way - the siege of The Sorcerer's Apprentice had ended.

In order for any investigative television programme to present an effective and dramatic expose, they need to produce a home grown British villain of the piece for the customary 'doorstepping'. In this instance, they mistakenly chose the wrong man as their victim. Although research had obviously shown that Chris Bray was innocent of any involvement with either paedophilia or Satanism, it was no doubt considered that as some of his previous media performances had been 'argumentative', doorstepping might provoke him into some good television material.

The idea was obviously to incite public hatred of the satanic stereotype and then direct all that venom at Chris Bray and his business operation. The researchers reasoned that, as an occultist, Chris Bray MUST be doing something wrong somewhere and even if his business was lawful, and he was innocent, it wouldn't matter to society if he was discredited and ruined. This reflected similar reasoning by the anti-occult campaigners who wanted Chris Bray and The Sorcerer's Apprentice off the scene because of what the shop represented; and even if he wasn't really involved in paedophilia, he was the Devil's agent and that justified any method at all.

For a programme ostensibly trying to expose 'satanic child-abuse', the accusations were pretty nonsensical. Chris Bray was accused of accepting an advertisement for funeral impedimenta, the suggestion inferring that The Sorcerer's Apprentice was trafficking in dead bodies! The business was accused of promoting Satanism but no mention was made of the fact that out of 3,500 different lines, the bookshop only stocked a handful that were directly related to Satanism. The idea was to force viewers to subconsciously link Chris and The Sorcerer's Apprentice with paedophilia via the emotional shock of the programme.

It worked very well. Delivery men refused to deliver; self-righteous graffiti artists daubed the outside of the building; trade suppliers of years' standing refused to trade; self-righteous customers stopped being customers; neighbours refused to be neighbourly and stopped Chris's daughter from playing with their children and for months afterwards, conversations would come to a stop mid-way, when it dawned who Chris was. Death threats over the telephone and through the mail were a regular occurrence.

For several weeks the local police kept the two bookshops under surveillance but in the early hours of Sunday, 13th August 1989, a week after the police withdrew, fanatics broke into Astonishing Books. They gained entry through a wire reinforced glass door and cut through 1" diameter security grills with bolt croppers. They hacked at and smashed bookshelves containing books on Witchcraft and Satanism and Crowley. They made a pile of these books, and these alone, in the centre of the shop, poured petrol over them, fired it and then left, taking nothing else.

Fortunately, ten minutes later, two customers were walking home and seeing the blaze, called the fire-brigade. The shop and most of its stock was gutted but the mail-order offices upstairs remained functional. It was something of a shock to discover 20 years of his life's work reduced to ashes within minutes; but there was no hesitation in Chris Bray's decision to rebuild what others had attempted to destroy. With the help of his dedicated staff working 16 hours a day, The Sorcerer's Apprentice was fully functional again within a week.

Unlike many occultists, Chris Bray does not cultivate an 'image' to promote his occult persona; he has the appearance of a successful business executive, which, of course, is exactly what he is. He has been slandered in the House of Commons; defamed by television companies and libelled by the press; he has been openly denounced by an M.P and child protection groups on radio, television and the national newspapers to such a degree, that the sheer volume of slander and libel makes any pursuit or redress through the courts impractical. Gangs of fundamentalists organised protests outside his shop and attempted to stop customers from entering the premises; and as well as death threats, there have been serious attempts to destroy his livelihood.

At times he can be an irascible and prickly character to deal with but circumstances such as these have forced him to take up the *oriflame* of occultism and enter the lists as its champion, because it was not only his staff who supported him and all he stood for. Those customers who had followed the victimisation from the beginning, looked upon the fire bombing as the last straw and spontaneously sent in cash to help him rebuild. The cash was put into a fund to pay for legal costs incurred in combating satanic hysteria.

That idea formalised into the Sub-Cultural Alternatives Freedom Foundation (S.A.F.F), a national organisation set up and financed by thousands of people (and not only occultists), to protect their freedom of belief. The S.A.F.F now exists to counter prejudice by bringing court action against people who infringe those rights and to offer specialist legal advice to those who suffer harassment. For the first time in history, occultists need not suffer persecution by vicious neighbours, unsympathetic friends or bigoted employers because they do not have the financial resources to fight back.

Chris is adamant that the need for the S.A.F.F was crucial. "Despite great efforts by a few hundred loyal members, the continuous lack of funding and idiotic suspicion from other occultists has always hampered what we could have achieved."

What the S.A.F.F has achieved has been immense against almost overwhelming odds. The organisation has grown up with the anti-occult campaign; has already made its own naive mistakes; understands democratic limitations; can detect government bureaucracy and has built up a power base of listening ears; a massive data base of information, photographs, tape recordings, news clippings, documents and other research resources which would normally take years to amass. The success of the S.A.F.F intelligence network has pulled off some impressive coups, as far as pre-empting fundamentalist influence on establishment bodies.

By March 1990, the S.A.F.F could really consider itself an organisation with a growing membership who were willing to act on directives received from S.A.F.F headquarters in Leeds. From all over the country, copies of radio tapes, newspaper cuttings and information were flooding into S.A.F.F HQ, ensuring that no article or interview that misrepresented occultism was allowed to pass without some form of complaint being registered against the editor or programme planners.

Early on in the campaign, a group of fundamentalist activists illegally reconstructed advertisements and leaflets belonging to a Lincoln occult shop, the Bridge of Dreams, to look as though the shop was passing itself off as The Sorcerer's Apprentice. By using parts from genuine Sorcerer's Apprentice listings and trademarked titles, the fundamentalists produced invitations for local occultists to visit the Bridge of Dreams. The idea was twofold: (a) to make a link with The Sorcerer's Apprentice and heighten local opposition to the Bridge of Dreams on the basis that The Sorcerer's Apprentice had been connected with paedophilia; and (b) to divide and occupy the enemy by sending samples of the forged leaflets to The Sorcerer's Apprentice, for they were well aware that Chris Bray dealt with any form of pirating by legal action.

The plan was to set one occultist against the other and, to this end, several forged leaflets and catalogues were sent anonymously to The Sorcerer's Apprentice. One of the activist group posed as a regular customer and telephoned to 'warn' The Sorcerer's Apprentice of the Bridge of Dreams' alleged pirating of The Sorcerer's Apprentice's trading name. As it happens, the confusion caused exactly the reverse - the Bridge of Dreams were already members of the S.A.F.F and had been working in close connection with S.A.F.F HQ as a result of vigorous fundamentalist campaigning against the Lincoln shop. Since smear tactics failed, on the night of 28th January 1991, arsonists petrol-bombed the Bridge of Dreams; again nothing was stolen - the motive was malice.

The majority of occultists and Pagans, however, safe within their own circle of friends, were unaware that one organisation was battling against almost insurmountable odds. The campaign against The Sorcerer's Apprentice lasted for over three years and although it has somewhat abated, it is far from over - the shop was paint-bombed with several 5 litre cans of white paint during June 1991. To outsiders however, the elements of a Christian fundamentalist campaign linking ritual abuse with the occult were merely typical examples of media sensationalism; they were unable to see the complete scope of the detailed strategy and the subtleties of the combined campaign perpetrated by the joint militia of religion and establishment.

Of course, Chris complained to just about everyone about the defamatory television reporting and took preliminary legal action but it didn't help because television investigative journalists are good at their jobs and to 12 million viewers, he WAS the fiendish child-abusing satanic criminal they had projected. The programme, however, received over a 100 independent complaints from British occultists concerned by the misrepresentation of the Craft and the large number forced the B.C.C to take action. Chris Bray lodged a personal complaint to the Broadcasting Complaints Commission *which was upheld and the programme makers admonished.* The second complaint that the programme had been misleading and unfair to occultism was (illogical) overruled.

[At this juncture, it is interesting to quote from a transcript of an instructional audio tape produced for one of the fundamentalist groups: "... when you see a programme on the TV which is of an occult nature, ring up and complain . That represents 50,000 viewers ... if ... you rang three times that would be 150,000 viewers. And if you got two other people to ring and complain, and those two got another two, it would have an impact because these people are only putting programmes on which the public are wanting. If the complaints outweighed those that wanted it then they would change the programme ... (sic)"

This illustrates to what levels the fundamentalists will stoop to prevent programmes being shown. All television companies determine complaints on a statistical basis. 10 or 15 people calling after a particular programme is considered representative of the total viewing audience for the programme. The television companies simply multiply up!]

Some well meaning occultists wrote to their local and national newspapers giving their alternative point of view but most were blissfully ignorant of the history behind the campaign. During this period Chris Bray kept a continuous correspondence with influential people in an attempt to stem the tide of religious fanaticism. He estimates that he had written several hundred letters (each averaging four pages) to all levels of government; newspaper editors; The Press Council; The I.B.A; The U.N Committee for Human Rights and challenged every publication or broadcast which perpetrated the occult-linked child-abuse allegations.

Despite the personal sacrifice, hardship and animosity, Chris Bray feels that the anti-occult campaign has revealed a completely new perspective on occultism in this country, both from without and within. The continuous crisis that threatened the community over the past three years has separated the genuine from the pseudos and underlined the lack of real commitment in some of the self-styled occult leaders.

He has even gone so far as to claim that Christian fundamentalists have done occultism a favour in that the popularisation of the occult in recent years had spawned many pseudos with soft underbellies; yuppy-occultists who are themselves misled and who subsequently mislead others. Corrupt occultists who are prepared to denigrate their oaths in favour of self-promotion, who find it easier to slander others rather than contribute something productive themselves. People, who faced with a bigger pond dived back into their own small pond, in order to blinker their eyes from events and create their own safe, cosy world within.

While the battle lines were being drawn early in 1988 and the anti-occult campaigners were calmly lining up pre-targeted victims ready for an outright onslaught, Chris watched active individuals with influence in occult/Pagan circles who kept themselves busy with: "The usual scenario of internecine squabbles and naive arguments over whether a Witch should use her knife or a sword to inscribe the magic circle, or whether the Fool should be numbered 0 or 22, or any of the million and one silly contentions that occultists seem plagued to indulge themselves in, to be able to opine their views in order to see their names in print."

The machinations of the S.A.F.F may have formed a hard core nucleus of committed occultists but it also exposed the lack of commitment on the part of many senior British practitioners. Even well-known authors of occult books who were receiving royalties from their publications; who incited others to follow their teachings, suddenly bowed out and refused to defend their own work when the going got tough. Chris has seen occult publishers, openly defamed by the fundamentalist press, refuse to get involved; and since authors and publishers such as these refuse to endorse the tenets and teachings which provide them with their incomes, The Sorcerer's Apprentice stopped selling their books.

He can also list three dozen examples of well-know occultists who turned and ran, or otherwise complicated the already complex proceedings in order to save their own jobs or reputations, which they apparently considered had priority over their integrity.

For the first two years of the campaign, Chris Bray had fought virtually single-handed, a continuous front-line war of attrition against a carefully formulated anti-occult campaign. However, since the inauguration of the S.A.F.F and with the help of other committed occult groups from all over the UK, S.A.F.F supporters were able to build up an impressive intelligence network and pre-empt a considerable amount of fundamentalist strategy.

The Siege of the Sorcerer's Apprentice was an important event in the history of modern occultism, although, at the time, very few people were aware of what was happening. The repercussions that followed the numerous television screenings of anti-occult propaganda are still being felt. Needless to say there have been repercussions that have come from unexpected quarters and one of those was another personal attempt to discredit Chris Bray in the eyes of the occult community. The S.A.F.F went out of its way to ensure that all its members were aware of the false accusations that were being levelled at certain individuals during the campaign; which makes it doubly incongruous that a further character assassination attempt came from a minority group whom Chris had been defending so vigorously.

So why was Chris Bray and The Sorcerer's Apprentice singled out for attack right from the beginning of the anti-occult campaign?

In Chris's own opinion, his business operation represented a microcosm of the occult in the UK and its evolution was an indicator of national importance. Being at the forefront, when people start slinging mud, The Sorcerer's Apprentice was always amongst the first to get hit. Because the shop openly sold half a dozen books and magazines on genuine Satanism, the business and its owner became the number one target on two levels. Firstly, the fundamentalists saw the mere existence of the business as living proof of the work of their antichrist (even though the shop sold more books on Christian Mysticism than Satanism) and secondly, fundamentalist leaders realised that if they allowed The Sorcerer's Apprentice to continue to present the GENUINE aspects of occultism, it could limited their control over public thinking.

There was also the added attraction of attacking a high personality profile and reputation. Possibly The Sorcerer's Apprentice is the best known supplier of occult books and artefacts in Europe and has never made any attempt to conceal its identity. In over 15 years of trading the business had built up a well deserved reputation for reliability and service. Neither did it conceal its activities behind an obscure warehouse address or mailbox number; the shops were there, on a busy road, for anyone to visit during normal opening hours. If such a reputable business could be implicated in the satanic hysteria, then other smaller businesses would be deemed guilty by association.

Towards the end of 1993 (five years after the Siege), interviewer

Tony Rhodes asked Chris why he'd ducked the television 'doorstepping' instead of taking the opportunity of repudiating the allegations.

Chris replied: "Only rarely are things as obvious, or foolish as they at first seem. You must remember that the media keep a viewer's focus purposefully narrow ... The story was simply one political step in a staircase of gambits by both the media and the fundamentalists to squeeze out every last drop of shock-horror from the 'satanic child-abuse' scare. Viewer's perspectives of the arguments involved seemed straight forward but in reality the situation was much more complex.

"I knew, even at this early juncture, that this was the first stage in a sea-change which would victimise a great many innocent people, permanently erode freedom of belief and the free passage of information. Even now, the rank-and-file occultist is oblivious to the dangers which exist. They have hardly any concept of the massive power and political influence of the fundamentalist machine; then there are the militants - I regularly receive death threats from such people.

"I knew the risks and I wasn't about to take any more; either for myself or my staff. The confusion and terror which such an assault brings with it is immense. The siege had gone on for hours. The police had been called but refused to do anything but escort us from the building. Customers were being harassed as they entered. Telephoto lenses were trained through the upstairs windows so we couldn't function without grovelling about on our hands and knees. We had to lock the door to stop them gaining entry. The staff were bemused and frightened.

"If the media could get away with this, legally, what would they do when we got outside? Provoke one of the lads in order to get a reaction? Follow us home, note our addresses and then terrorise us again another day? I had to make a decision to break this circle of victimisation; all my staff are very committed people, but none of us deserved this. So I broke out the Halloween vampire masks in order to confuse the issue and avoid identification. Under the circumstances (and with the benefit of hindsight) it was the best thing to do; the fact that our premises were firebombed by religious fanatics several weeks afterwards rather underlines that point."

Realising that he was treading on glass, Tony Rhodes pressed home the doubt that some people had expressed over whether the arson was, in fact, the work of militant fundamentalists.

Chris was quick to reply: "It's bad enough having 20 years of your life's work turned to ashes overnight, to have to justify yourself to people afterwards adds insult to injury. I get angry because the same people who challenge me for conclusive evidence of my statements about the fire are usually the very same people who are prepared to accept satanic abuse allegations at face value! There were at least two perpetrators. It was premeditated; they had been before to size up our security and brought specialist tools with them to break through the security grills. The police kept up protective surveillance of the property for a few weeks but the arsonists struck a week or so after this was lifted.

"Once inside they attacked bookshelves on the right hand side which contained books on Crowley, then they attacked the bookshelves on the other side of the shop containing books on Witchcraft. They chopped and hit at the shelves with something heavy ... as though axed through. They scooped up these books, and these books only, off the shelves and built a pyre of them in the centre of the shop about three feet tall. Then they set fire to them all, leaving without taking anything. Nothing else was touched; not even the float in the till. Robbery was not the motive."

Nevertheless, Chris Bray felt it provident to close the Astonishing Books operation after the fire because he realised that the shop would be in danger of being burnt down every time it was rebuilt. Astonishing Books had been 'an experiment in open-heart surgery which had failed' according to its owner. Because of the limited ground floor space at The Sorcerer's Apprentice, it could not cater for browsing customers; also critics were suggesting that as the windows of the shop were blacked out and members of the public were not allowed inside, something sinister must be hidden away behind the darkened facade.

The windows had been boarded over *because self-righteous religious fanatics kept on kicking them in,* Chris remembers, but he took the critics at their word and decided to open a bright and airy new shop which would provide calling clients with an opportunity to browse and show that there was nothing to hide. He realises now that he was being naive because those who criticised the business for being boarded up and blacked out wanted it that way.

"The new shop was opened during the summer of 1985 in a very high profile position which fuelled the insecurity of local fundamentalists ... they take it as a challenge and hound you out, or burn you down. Banished to a lowly back-street position, they can then point the finger of guilt and say, 'We told you so - these are low-lifes who do not want to be part of 'decent' society; they have something to hide and should be shunned.' All (occult) shops which are run on genuine lines are at risk," he concluded.

In attempting to mobilise British occultists against the threat of fundamentalism, Chris Bray has made enemies. There are those who scoffed at his original warnings; those who took offence at being told they were not doing enough to support the S.A.F.F; those who believed that 'there was no smoke without fire' in the accusations levelled against him and backed away. All have been proved wrong and everything that Chris Bray warned against has come to pass . The blade, having been tempered in the fires of fundamentalist hatred, has emerged with an even finer cutting edge.

Chapter 10: Media Inquisition

Use of the printed word to inflame the populace against Witchcraft is not a new idea. By the time Caxton's printing press had revolutionised people's access to reading matter, there were those ready to use the new contraption for more ominous purposes. Graphic pamphlets containing the confessions of Witches helped to promote the Witch-hysteria across the country, culminating in localised support for the Witchfinders. And, as with the present day's sensational journalism which inflamed the anti-occult campaign out of all proportion, blame can be laid squarely at the doors of the authors of those early pamphlets who were responsible for inciting normal, average citizens to commit acts of persecution against their neighbours.

In an open letter to readers of the *Lamp of Thoth* magazine Michael Howard, advised those involved in the Craft to 'Put Your House In Order' and outlined the cruel, hard facts concerning trafficking with the media:

"A BBC television researcher recently asked me if I could introduce her to some normal Pagans. We were driving back to my local station having spent a pleasant afternoon with a nice Pagan couple who were very much into ecology, anti-nukes and self sufficiency but who she regarded as a little 'hippyish'. When I asked her to define what a 'normal' Pagan was (having never encountered such an animal in the wild myself) she replied that, ideally, she wanted a High Court Judge or Bank Manager who was willing to go public with his Pagan beliefs! Such is the naivety of the media, which is sometimes paralleled by those within the occult/Pagan movement, who criticise those who refuse to come out.

"From my own personal experience, I certainly would not criticise anyone who did not feel they wanted to expose themselves and their family to the often cynical scrutiny of the media. Refusal to do so is not in my opinion a stance which can be derided as showing any lack of spiritual conviction in Pagan beliefs - in fact, if anything it is the opposite.

"Personally I have no wish either to be associated with the many self-appointed spokespersons who claim to represent the Old Ways in the public eye. Neither do I relish the thought of being associated with Satanists, child molesters, neo-Nazis, etc. or be characterised as an 'emotionally disturbed dropout who cannot cope with modern technological society', which are some of the labels pinned on all (occultists) in media reports. Anyone who believes they can have editorial control over interviews or news stories after the journalist involved leaves their home is, quite frankly, living in cloud-cuckoo-land.

"The establishment of organisations to promote a better image of Paganism *vis-a-vis* the media are a waste of time and energy. Since I first became involved in the Pagan movement in the early 1960s, there have been numerous attempts to unify Pagans or promote a better image. These have failed for a variety of reasons, not the least because Paganism (like the occult *per se*) attracts more than its fair share of cranks, exhibitionists and con-men.

"We are not supposed to say this but if you have been around a long time you will recognise it as a fact. Because of the high profile of this type of person, they tend to attract media coverage because basically they make a good story. That is all the average media hack is ultimately after. Journalists do not give a shit about the spiritual aspects of the Old Ways and - to be 100% honest - neither do many (not all, of course) of the Witches and Pagans they interview."

Since 1988 the amount of coverage given to occult-bashing by the media has reached new heights of sensationalism and, in the main, endorses those views made many years ago by Michael Howard. Anton Lavey, who has had more than his fair share of media attention believes there was more factual, more informed reporting going on in 1975 than there is now:

"Of course, there's more money and attention in being a professional hysteric now, making a living telling your masturbatory fantasies on nationwide television. There are people on the talk-show circuit who claim to be ex-members or ex-priests from a satanic organisation who can't even show they read the same book I wrote, let alone give an accurate rendition of our practices and philosophy. It's funny that they're always 'High Priests', there are never any 'Low Priests' or just plain 'Priests'. There were never any 'High Priests' until I came along, except in Puccini operas."

Despite the lurid testimonies of such repentant converts who revealed how they escaped the clutches of black covens after witnessing the most appalling sacrifices and murders, not one of them has been able to provide the evidence to justify a police investigation. The victims can remember in graphic, technicolour detail the most horrendous acts, even down to the last drop of spilt blood - but suffer from total amnesia when it comes down to places, dates and names of those instigating the satanic acts in question. Realising that the claims would not be taken seriously without something more concrete to offer, the survivors were encouraged to introduce the threat of 'satanic child-abuse' - the idea for which had been conceived from information coming in from America - and the fundamentalist conspiracy to undermine occultism was underway.

In 1989 *ORCRO Magazine (The Occult Response to the Christian Response to the Occult)* was able to make the following report to its readers: "During the year, a group of loosely connected people began telling newspapers increasingly ghoulish stories about how satanic cults were luring children into the occult. Teenage girls were being deliberately made pregnant in order that the aborted foetus could be used for sacrifice. The first suspected cases to be investigated by social workers and police appeared like a rash in late 1988 in Kent, Nottingham and Cheshire. In Nottingham nine adults were later jailed for sex offences against children but nowhere did the police investigation uncover any evidence of satanic practices or involvement."

Looking back over the mountain of newspaper and magazine cuttings in the S.A.F.F archive it is unbelievable just how many column inches were devoted to promoting satanic hysteria without one scrap of factual evidence to support it. Obviously there is little that can be done about those posing as occult 'experts' and the counterattack mounted by occult organisations was seriously curtailed by the negative attitude shown by editors and programme makers towards genuine practioners. Any snippet that could carry a banner-headline containing certain occult 'buzz-words' was featured prominently as the media cashed-in on the mounting satanic hysteria.

Despite the efforts of the S.A.F.F, The Pagan Federation and various other individuals, there were also a series of media performances by some Pagans that were downright detrimental to the Craft. One programme featured a group whose lunatic sylvan caperings were an embarrassment to any self-respecting Crafter. Another coven told the television interviewer that on Samhain (Halloween) they would be using the festival as an opportunity to pray for world peace! A well meant sentiment, perhaps, but still presenting a totally inaccurate and misleading representation of the religious significance of Samhain to the public.

While the fundamentalists were chalking up their success with the media, three conferences on ritual abuse for social workers, police officers, psychotherapists and other child-care groups took place during April and September 1989. At one conference held in Reading, a Nottingham senior social worker erroneously stated that their child-abuse cases involved a satanic ring, even though police evidence showed the contrary.

Of course there were some social workers who were extremely concerned about the influence of the fundamentalist 'experts'. One senior social worker who had attended the conference held at Reading University, was totally unconvinced by the claims. "I have never heard such gobbledgook in all my life. I heard the most amazing tales of sorcery and Witchcraft but there was never one solid fact to back it up."

The three day conference took place amid secrecy which 'almost amounted to paranoia' stated one delegate. The Chairman first of all asked if the Press were present. When there was no response, delegates were then required to identify themselves individually. There were more than 250 people present representing social workers, police, probation officers and N.S.P.C.C staff.

Delegates were handed a printed list of 'satanic indicators' compiled by an America expert (since discredited in the USA) on child-abuse, which listed things they should look for when questioning children. It ranged from physical details, such as missing fingertips, to psychological indicators such as bed wetting, blowing raspberries, wild laughter and an abnormal interest in death. Leaving nothing to chance, the satanic indicators were also distributed to nearly every police force, and although many might regard them as absurd, the Social Services Inspectorate sent similar memoranda *to every social services department in Britain.*

Another social worker attending the conference said: "The longer this went on the more sceptical I became. Where was the proof? Where were the bodies? But I admit I did not have the courage to get to my feet and voice my doubts. Everyone was taking copious notes. There was an atmosphere of hysteria around which I found frightening."

During 1990 the biggest set back to those campaigning to present the occult in a reasonable light, were the revelations in the national press that the N.S.P.C.C's annual report showed a concern over 'satanic child-abuse'. Further investigations proved that the annual report did NOT mention anything of the kind, however, the N.S.P.C.C's press release, given out on the 12th April 1990 did - but not as the great earth shattering issue as the public were led to believe.

Briefly, the press release stated that: "The N.S.P.C.C has voiced its increasing concern as evidence is mounting of child pornography, ritualistic abuse and sex rings involving children ... emotional abuse of children in bizarre ceremonies. An increasing number of N.S.P.C.C teams are working with children who have been ritualistically abused. A great deal more needs to be found out about the scale of the problem."

But as *ORCRO Magazine* pointed out to its readers: "Ritualistic abuse is of course a meaningless term. Any series of customarily repeated acts is 'ritualistic'. Most sexual abuse is 'ritualistic' in as much as there is a definite pattern that is followed. The persistent misuse of the word with its overtones of dark forces helps no one. To bring in religious overtones when the weight of verified, documented, available evidence and academic opinion suggests that there is no case to answer, is to confuse the issue and to invite the diversion of resources for no good reason - unless the suppression of alternative religions is a good reason!"

Although the lack of evidence for these claims did not prevent the majority of newspapers from compromising accuracy by printing the sleaziest stories they could find, *The Yorkshire Post* of 13th March 1990 tried to offer some degree of rationality:

"It would be most unfortunate were excitable talk of rituals and sacrifices to distract attention from the more prevalent forms of child-abuse. There is clear evidence for example, of the way in which children have been lured into sex rings, often involving parents or close relatives. What is also evident is that the quantity of child pornography is now in circulation. It makes more sense to tackle those known evils before addressing new and somewhat speculative apprehensions."

The tide began to turn on 12th August 1990, when *The Independent on Sunday* ran Rosie Waterhouse's 'The Making of a Satanic Myth' which refused to swallow any more fundamentalist prating and satanic hysteria without any evidence to support the claims. The Rochdale scandal broke in the newspapers at the beginning of September, revealing that children had been snatched from their beds at 7 o'clock in the morning and placed in care; the parents were subsequently silenced by an injunction that prevented them talking about their experiences to anyone outside the court, ie. councillors, outside lobbyists and the media.

On 9th September *The Mail on Sunday* unleashed its own indignant attack by running a double page spread, emphasising the plight of the families involved. It was a breakthrough for occultism, but far too late to prevent the spread of a myth that showed little concern about the misery inflicted on innocent families. The majority of accused parents had no more interest in occultism than watching the late night horror movie, or reading the latest James Herbert bestseller, but the warmth and security of their family group had been irreparably damaged by the slur of investigation. The children had been badly traumatised by their ordeal and the psychological repercussions to both parent and child were incalculable.

By 12th September, *Radio 4* had raised the question of a fundamentalist conspiracy and suggested that paedophiles were now using 'satanic child-abuse' as a smokescreen to cover their own activities, offering the theory that they now purposefully cloaked the abuse with ritual so that the victim's stories were so bizarre that they would not be believed. The case was offered of a two year old who claimed to have been abused by a lion. When it was investigated, it transpired that the accused had dressed up as a lion to guarantee the bizarreness of the claim, and, of course, at first the child was not believed.

Child psychologist Elisabeth Newson, who acted as consultant in the ritual abuse investigations in Nottingham, aired her belief that many social workers had been over-influenced by what they had heard about the phenomena at the professional conferences. She also believed in the possibility of a direct link between the conferences and the then current mania for exposing alleged 'satanic child-abuse'. She was quoted as saying: "Social workers are under pressure to have learned something from conferences. People in their department refer to them for advice, so they become expert. The situation is self perpetuating. They come across examples, then they are the speakers at the next conference. This means they have a very strong commitment to believing in it - their reputation is on the line."

By this time, however, social workers themselves had also fallen victim to the myth and been duped into active participation in a prolonged bout of what amounted to nothing more than religious persecution. Many have since come under fire as a result of their enthusiasm to remove children from the family home; some have no doubt been disciplined; others have lost their jobs as a result and many parents are now seeking legal advice. So discredited were the satanic implications that even the usually reserved tone of *The Sunday Times* changed on 30th September 1990 by repeating a joke that was doing the rounds in Rochdale: What, they were asking, is the difference between a rottweiler and a social worker? Answer: There's an outside chance you might get your children back from a rottweiler.

In reply to the article 'Children Speared on the Horns of a Demonic Dilemma' by Bryan Appleyard in *The Sunday Times*, the Chief Executive of Rochdale Metropolitan Council concluded by stating: "I had hoped that the serious media would treat these matters in an intelligent way." For the first time in three years the 'serious media' WAS beginning to develop a more sceptical view of the satanic claims and the Chief Exec. had found himself dangling on the end of his own fundamentalist primed hook.

Fortunately for British Paganism, the police were not dragged into this whirlpool of fanaticism and fantasy. In an exclusive interview with *The Independent on Sunday,* Dan Crompton, the Chief Constable of Nottinghamshire, expressed his anger that a team of social workers should continue to make claims that exhaustive investigations by police and other social workers had been unable to corroborate with hard evidence; and that the programme makers should sensationalise such allegations by accusing the police of failing to investigate thoroughly. He revealed that he would be sending a confidential internal report to the Home Secretary, David Waddington, to 'kill off once and for all' stories that children from Nottingham had been victims of satanic abuse.

There can no doubt that some children suffer appalling sexual abuse, as 23 children did in the Nottingham case - eight members of their family and an adult friend were jailed in January 1989 for vile offences in circumstances that the judge described as a 'vortex of evil'. Months after the children were taken into care they began to talk about Witchcraft and satanic ceremonies but again the police found no supporting evidence. As *The Independent on Sunday* revealed, the stories of Witches and monsters, babies and blood, started only AFTER play techniques were introduced into the questioning of the children by social workers from the N.S.P.C.C.

Criticising the way social workers interviewed children in Nottingham, Mr Crompton said: "Disclosure work needs to be tightly controlled. Leading questions, prompting, making suggestions to the child can seriously contaminate evidence."

Professors John and Elisabeth Newson, psychologists who were asked to assess the techniques used at Nottingham, concluded that one 17 year old girl 'was led to confabulate' a story that she had taken part in satanic sacrifices. The girl later said the story was totally untrue and that: "The only knowledge that she had, had come from social workers , that she had been pressurised, that the social workers would not take no for an answer."

Throughout the rest of 1990 and 1991, *The Mail on Sunday* kept up the pressure by devoting double and triple page articles exposing the lunacy behind the claims of satanic hysteria. On the 7th October 1990 they reported that the 'Satan Case Inquiry Damns Social Workers' and revealed that government guidelines had been flouted by social workers and, by the 21st October, the newspaper revealed that having spent many weeks investigating the claims and counter-claims, they had little doubt where the truth lay: *While there may be some individuals who cloak their activities with satanic overtones, the concept of a highly organised network was nonsense - and dangerous nonsense at that.* Because of the 'satanic child-abuse' controversy, the newspaper reported, the relationship between police and social workers had totally broken down 'through professional jealousy', degenerating into sheer hatred and venom.

As social workers came under increasing pressure, both from the serious media and the courts, to justify their severe action in taking children into care, the term 'satanic abuse' had been quietly replaced with the less emotive 'ritual abuse'. In fact the two were now indistinguishable in the public mind and the anti-occult campaign plotted by the fundamentalists had caused irretrievable differences between the very people who should be working together to stamp out paedophilia. During the later stages of the case, social workers withdrew all allegations concerning 'satanic abuse' but, by then, the damage inflicted upon the occult community was too far advanced to be ignored.

But why did the media allow the truth to be distorted to fit ghoulish sensationalism without first checking the facts?

The S.A.F.F maintained that the media find fabricated stories just as sensational as the original anti-occult propaganda. Also such stories are cheap. No costly bribes for the gaff; the reporter need not even get up from his desk, as the fundamentalist press officers will supply pictures, statements and such like through the post. Quotes are readily given over the telephone and willing survivors are always available for interview. The media will not cease its interest, said a spokesperson, because after panning the occult for the past three years, and defaming many occultists, they have realised that none of those involved have the financial resources needed to take legal action.

Because the media ignored all attempts to present the occult side of the argument, the S.A.F.F implemented a policy of by-passing the British press; normal press-releases and information broadsheets were sent out every few weeks to update individuals and authorities embroiled in satanic hysteria. S.A.F.F documents were constantly 'devalued' although the information contained in them was always deadly accurate and of immense importance to the enquiries. Despite the unequivocal evidence and factual documentary proof the S.A.F.F amassed, which proved that the ritual abuse allegations were pure fabrication, they knew that a Rochdale had to occur sooner or later. The sad fact is that nobody listened to their warnings.

As Chris Bray relates: "Our continuous attempts to get someone, *anyone*, to come and look at the evidence we held, met a total and utter wall of ignorance and prejudice which was unbelievable in its scope."

As long ago as 1988 he was assiduously writing to the Government, the police, M.Ps and Social Services. He complained to them about misrepresentation, lies, intolerance, corruption, incitement and the fundamentalist origins of the anti-New Age campaign. He named names and he named motives. He gave times and dates, always providing documentary evidence to prove his case. He sent every one of those letters *by recorded delivery and can prove the receipt* - and the lack of response of every person who read them.

Chris Bray was under no illusions as to the position of the S.A.F.F in establishment circles - it was looked upon as an association of the same twisted, criminal, dishonourable and antisocial occultists that were involved in Satanism and was not to be trusted. It was apparent that the S.A.F.F wasn't getting the truth across as quickly as the fundamentalists were drumming up the lies. Following the continuous stream of individual and personal letters to MPS, police constables and social workers, the S.A.F.F embarked upon a blanket dissemination of factual evidence in the form of thousands of newsletters. It is still hard for them to believe that whilst they kept up a constant barrage of accurate information, hundreds of influential people glibly ignored it.

On a repetitive and regular basis they mailed out to the following people:

1. Every national newspaper and provincial editor whose newspaper had at any time featured any article promoting satanic hysteria.

2. Every chief journalist and freelance writer who had at any time written about the ritual-abuse allegations.

3. Every chief constable of every police force in the UK and every police constable (they knew of) who had undertaken 'satanic child-abuse' investigations.

4. Every government department which had an interest in the ongoing situation and every person in those departments who they had previously written personal letters to.

5. Every one of the hundreds of M.Ps in Parliament.

6. Every Director of Social Services in every locality in the UK.

7. Every body or group which had been associated with the scare (ie. N.S.P.C.C, Childline, Childwatch, Amnesty International, United Nations Association, etc)

8. Every broadcasting body, radio station, television company and the people who had produced programmes which had upheld or investigated the 'satanic child-abuse' hoax.

In short, literally thousands of these newsletters reached the most influential and concerned people in this matter nationally. These constant and repetitive press releases were further supplemented by other groups similar to the S.A.F.F who distributed their own findings on the bogus nature of the anti-occult campaign. Amongst these were The Pagan Federation and particularly the independent *Bad News* pamphlet, published by John Freedom, who had unlimited access to the S.A.F.F correspondence files.

Nevertheless there are those on the fringes of occultism who use the media to promote an image of self-grandiosity and infuriate genuine practitioners by giving practical demonstrations of their total ignorance of initiated occultism. When one well-known *media-darling* appeared on television, she repeatedly used the Craft blessing 'Blessed Be' on non-Crafters and telephone callers, totally oblivious to the fact that it is a blessing of the Goddess *only made to those who have undergone initiation*; explaining that it was the Craft equivalent of saying 'hello' and 'goodbye'. She then repeated 'Blessed Be' at the finale to a ridiculous spell, instead of the traditional 'So mote it be'.

If these antics were not sufficient to disprove any assertion about her own ability as a Witch, the spell itself did. This was a love-spell worked for two people already in love, which she worked at the wrong hour, on the wrong day, on the wrong phase of the moon, *using someone else's hair* to bind the dolls (because it is 'only symbolic') and which she consecrated in the studio by appealing to Mars instead of Venus. "In short," added a disgusted S.A.F.F. spokesman, "a total travesty from the figmented mind of an utter beginner!"

This person is occult illiterate. She is *not* a witch and although she had claimed to be a Wiccan, the Wiccan community deny this emphatically; yet within the space of six months she was catapulted into the centre of attention and called upon by the media whenever an 'occult expert' was needed. As the spokesman for the S.A.F.F explained: "If there was anyone NOT EQUIPPED to plead the Witches' case it is this quisling pretender who befriends and assists our adversaries to effect her own aggrandisement and safety. Because she has set herself up as a spokesperson for the Craft, her silliness must be punctured at every opportunity, lest she misleads newcomers and others with her idiocy."

The success of the counterattack against fundamentalist propaganda has not been without its casualties. There have been several instances of well-meaning Pagans who suffered a severe mauling by the press, as happened in the case of Stephen from Blackburn. During the height of the satanic hysteria, Stephen decided to help counter some of the bad publicity about occultism by contacting the editor of his local newspaper. In his naivety, he laboured under the misapprehension that because he was innocent of any sinister practices, that he would be fairly dealt with.

The editor affirmed that space would be made available to allow him to tell the truth about Paganism but when the article appeared, it was run alongside a full page article of anti-occult propaganda; Stephen's photograph and story were used in a manner that twisted his occult involvement out of all proportion. As a result Stephen became the victim of so much abuse that he contacted the editor again, and asked him for a right of reply. He was ignored. The persecution built up to such a degree that the still-hopeful Pagan decided to call on the editor in person. All his attempts were thwarted and in his frustration, Stephen made certain idiotic threats to burn the newspaper to the ground. He also sent a tape threatening to throw acid, and at this stage the police were called in. As a result, Stephen found himself in court, found guilty and forced to take psychiatric treatment.

Commenting on the case, Chris Bray said: "Stephen's actions might seem rather extreme to the armchair reader but let me tell you that the pressures and frustrations which occur when such persecution takes place, and the very real damage it does to employment, career prospects, relations with the family, neighbours and friends is something which pushes ordinary and honest people into earthing their frustrations."

Chris had no doubt that Stephen would not have carried out any of his threats; but the judge disagreed and found him guilty. He hadn't done anything wrong. He had tried to be truthful and honest and, in doing so, was tricked and framed into being publicly associated with 'satanic child-abuse'. A scare he knew didn't exist anyway. This association caused him endless persecution from thugs and neighbours, at work, etc. He took reasonable steps to try to obtain justice and fair-play. *The people who set him up denied him that platform, knowing very well that he was innocent.* In an attempt to present himself personally to try and convince the editor, he was ridiculed and frustrated. At that point, having absolutely no method open to him to obtain vindication, he made a couple of silly statements and is persecuted even further, by being slurred with the possibility of being mentally unstable or dangerous - and enforced to undergo psychiatric examination. The S.A.F.F wrote to him offering to supply him with information to launch an appeal, but the poor chap is now so crushed by the system, and disillusioned with the inability of the judiciary to mete out justice, that he refused any help.

But it is not just interviews that can be twisted to produce another sensational news item. *The Sunday Times* reported that even the famous Mori Poll was forced to complain publicly about the way social workers had distorted a poll that carefully distinguished trivia (such as someone under 16 being spoken to in an erotic way) from trauma, and found that one girl in every 220 had suffered serious sexual abuse in the family. Social workers had lumped all Mori's categories together and hysterically claimed that one girl in 10 was sexually abused in the family!

The S.A.F.F has since reported that a number of journalists were beginning to contact them and show an interest in the occult side of the story, but this is still an uphill struggle. They have also been approached by a number of freelance journalists who wish to tell the true story behind the satanic hysteria but the organisation remains sceptical. Since many of the regular national journalists who have expressed an interest in the behind-the-scenes story have been keen to project the blame for the hysteria on pseudo-political sources, the S.A.F.F do not believe there is a genuine desire to print the truth.

"This is a very important issue" says Chris Bray, "In the minds of 98% of the general public, 'satanic child-abuse' is a reality and Witches and Satanists are equally guilty. The propaganda has worked and ancient lies have been reinforced in their subconscious:

Even though there has never been a shred of evidence to prove it.
Even though there has not been one prosecution which confirms it.
Even though all cases so far investigated have been proved bogus.

The public know that Pagans and Witches murder babies and sexually abuse children. The only possible way that the occult can overcome these lies is if the media who were directly responsible for them, admit that it was a hoax and exonerate us completely."

Chapter 11:   An Unholy War

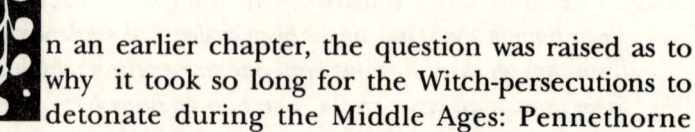

In an earlier chapter, the question was raised as to why it took so long for the Witch-persecutions to detonate during the Middle Ages: Pennethorne Hughes gave the reason that it had been extremely difficult to define the opposition that posed the threat to Rome. Chris Bray suggests that the orthodox Churches of the late 1980's had found themselves in a similar predicament.

Since the 1950s, the establishment hold on individual consciousness had loosened and the cult of individuality came to the fore. The much vaunted '60s did a lot of damage to both the establishment and the Church, because the benign revolution of the '60s gave each person the freedom to experiment with alternative beliefs, discover the real Self and build their own hotline to cosmic knowledge, using a mix of religious alternatives.

So fractionalised was this growth in spiritual freedom, that identifying it as a movement was difficult; each movement developed, apogeed and declined so rapidly that it became clear, with hindsight, that it was really a reflection of some greater current aimed at releasing individuality and originality. This current overturned social taboos and in the process, undermined the edifice of the establishment.

A product of the times, Chris Bray can look back on the beginnings of the revolutionary youth movements which, by qualification, always conflicted with authority's status quo. These movements were given much bad press and projected as anti- social:

Teddy boys, rock 'n' roll, beatniks, abstract art, Hell's Angels, Mersey Beat, The Beatles, transcendental meditation, yoga, Carnaby Street, flower power, Hare Krishna, hippies, Mods and Rockers, the Aquarian Age and Leary's Psychedelia, the occult explosion, skinheads, rock musicals and the pop culture ...
... all attempts to find and communicate expressions of individuality in a new order.

The threat of nuclear war had made the promises of religion redundant and the effects of democracy irrelevant. Along with these experimental expressions of individuality came political philosophies to match, and people began taking personal responsibility for the environment with embryonic conservation groups and 'back to the land' communes becoming prevalent. In short - people liberated themselves.

Such rebellion against established order continued unabated and saw the emergence of Heavy Metal music, Punks, Goths, etc. continuing as adaptations and modifications of the original current. Although the overworked term 'Aquarian Age' means less now than it did in the '60s, Chris observed, its significance, the death of Piscean attributes and the flowering of Aquarian concepts in a new age of optimism was clear to all, but in the '80s the current was again modified by subsequent generations and retitled the *New Age*.

To occultists and liberal minded people, like Chris Bray and Michael Howard who see the New Age as epitomising all that is best for humanity, it accords individuals their own sense of responsibility, the wisdom to live their own life, and evolve in their own particular and unique way, free from interference and unnecessary restriction. But, in Chris's own words, this is a bold philosophy and one that frightens the insecure. Many of those who identify with the Christian culture are steeped in perceptions which seem diametrically opposed to New Age ideals. Theirs is a paternal, restrictive, dogmatic and suppressive world-view, which cannot justify itself alongside New Age concepts. Christianity was losing the battle against a phantom which it could not define.

Therefore, the New Age had to be discredited and destroyed but it took fundamentalists years to mull this conclusion around; digest the various strands of it and come up with a holistic presentation of their enemy. *The Christian World News*, in an article (18th May 1990) stated that: "One of the reasons why New Age teaching has grown is the failure of the Church to provide for the spiritual hunger that abounds in our day. But like gnosticism, it poses a major threat to the Church. It represents a serious and fundamental challenge to the Christian world view. It offers a phony salvation and a false messiah." The Church's answer to Gnosticism was, of course, suppression by any means possible!

The present target of fundamentalism is the occult and while there are those Christians who may fool themselves into thinking that Witches and Satanists are the enemy, in reality fundamentalism will continue to repress *anything and everything* that represents New Age thinking. According to *The Mail on Sunday's* 'Analysis' report, signs of a family's occult involvement included ferns or palms in the home, human or animal bones, ritual books and diaries, medallions with satanic symbols and other occult jewellery, masks and costumes, posters of heavy metal or punk rock stars, paraphernalia and clothing associated with the martial arts and school composition books! How many homes in Britain or America do not possess one or more of those 'occult symbols'?

Even with the spectres of Nottingham, Cleveland, Rochdale and Orkney still fresh in the public mind, Chris Bray does not believe that there is any point in expecting influential people (however intellectual) to be able to distinguish between the finer points of scam and reality. But fortunately, the police force refused to become embroiled in the net of satanic hysteria and the social workers who had fallen under their influence.

The S.A.F.F was relieved to receive a request for a meeting from two Detective Inspectors from a North of England force, in order to give themselves a wider perspective into genuine occultism. The result of the four and a half hour discussion was to reveal the total ignorance of the police concerning true occult ideals, having been supplied only with fundamentalist information. One comment from the policemen stated: "We just can't believe that other police forces haven't come to talk to you - you've explained more in a couple of hours than we have been able to glean from months of enquiry."

Looking carefully at the above keywords of the Fifties, Sixties and

Seventies, Chris feels that it is possible to see exactly which things are targeted for suppression by the fundamentalist campaigners. They may pick the most *extreme* examples of Heavy Metal; the most *outrageous* examples of crooked cults; the most *terrible* case of mental disturbance brought about by hypnosis; the most *deplorable* misdiagnosis by alternative healers; and the most *fearful* crime carried out by someone who CLAIMS to be an occultist. In doing so they are attempting to substantiate the proposition that ALL aspects of the New Age are inherently antisocial, thereby working on the premise that by producing one pink elephant, will prove that all herds of elephants are pink!

S.A.F.F research highlights fundamentalist allegations and scares concerning occultism as falling into four different categories:

1. The organised sexual abuse of children and adults with links into pornographic markets.
2. The sacrifice and torture of humans.
3. The sacrifice and torture of animals.
4. A global satanic crime conspiracy involving extortion, blackmail, white slavery, pornography and drug trafficking.

The fundamentalists also maintain that these aims are fulfilled by recruitment and infiltration via the following 'doorways':

(i) Pop occultism accessed by the young, ie. astrology, fortune telling, tarot, ouija boards, psychic fayres and occult shops.

[They believe that EVERYONE involved in occultism, whether diviner or sorcerer, has a fealty to Satan and is obliged to route youngsters to the hard occult 'doorways' where they end up being tortured, abused, drugged and ultimately sacrificed. They also assert that there is a well-planned and orchestrated web of intrigue, which consciously directs newcomers to the occult through soft-occultism (magazines and psychic fayres), into hard core occult groups and satanic temples. Drawing no distinction between Witchcraft and Satanism (for they believe that both exist as part of the Devil's melting pot), they link Wicca and neo-Paganism with devil worship although there is no proof to substantiate these claims.]

(ii) The Rock Music industries are supposedly run by satanic 'god-fathers' who purposefully promote salacious images and hypnotise teenagers with 'backward masking' - subliminal messages digitally encoded and reversed, and included in Heavy Metal tracks.

[No fundamentalist has yet been able to provide proof of backward masking, although one organisation specialises in taking Heavy Metal tracks, digitising them, reversing, altering frequency, tone, cadence, decoding and rephrasing. Neither have they explained why the courts are not chock-a-block with Heavy Metal fans being prosecuted for psychopathic crimes. But the most damning indictment of all, is how backward masking investigators are immune from the subliminal commands which enforce irresistible criminal action in others!]

Anton Lavey, however, is disdainful of modern rock music, which he sees as part of the current de-sensitizing and de-emotionalising trend; and as for the links between rock music and Satanism in the form of 'Black Metal'- there is no association between the two.

"Actually," he says, "Satanic symbology is the only thing that has kept rock music alive for the past few years ... Kids buy records as badges of affiliation now. They say themselves that they don't listen to the words, they just like what the visuals communicate - and Satanic imagery is the most dramatic ... The music industry had nothing else to sell so they reached for the most powerful icon they could think of - Satanism. But all these bands ... stridently deny charges that they are advocating actual Devil worship. It's all in fun. It's the old story of using the Devil's name to make your millions, but not wanting to play the Devil's game.

"Satanic music is *not* heavy metal rock and rock," confirms Blanche Barton in his biography. "The real Satanic influence is seen in the revival of the lyrical, evocative music that Anton Lavey, an accomplished musician, has been playing all his life."

(iii) Fundamentalists claim that soft occult magazines are a recruiting ground for hard occultism and a curious interest in fortune telling or spiritualism, inevitably leads to contact with satanic elements.

(iv) Fourth on the list the fundamentalists place the infiltration of institutions and education thereby providing satanic elements with positions of influence in the professions and social services, enabling them to gain surreptitious access to children. There are, they assert, satanic conspirators who are teachers, policemen, doctors, nurses and social workers.

[This is a clever ploy. Firstly, it generates a state of paranoia in which those with any New Age interest would not dare to reveal it and secondly, those with genuine knowledge of occultism are effectively silenced. Each and every Halloween they mount a campaign to press local schools into banning Halloween mask making and drawings. If the headmaster/mistress disagrees, then they lobby the local Director of Education and the press. They usually get what they want.]

(v) The fundamentalist's conspiracy theory also applies very neatly to their greatest ally - the media. They suggest that production staff and journalists continually work to represent New Age ideals, employing an unnatural interest in hypnosis, meditation, visualisation and the supernatural to hook youngsters and the impressionable into darker, satanic realms.

[The hidden question in this argument is, of course, "Is it possible for a television or radio programme to force individuals to commit crimes against their will in the first place?" There is no doubt about the power of the media over an individual viewer/listener's perception, and Chris Bray personally believes that television DOES precipitate detrimental and sometimes criminal actions. However, this is an entirely different issue to the allegations being made by the fundamentalists, who state that the depicting of New Age ideals is MORE likely to result in antisocial behaviour or mental instability, than the usual mix of sex and violence which hits the screens on a repetitive basis. In this instant, anti-occultists are hijacking the inherent dangers in broadcasting and blaming it on the occult.]

On 12th June 1990, an article by Debbie Nathan in *Voice* magazine challenged the 'Ritual Sex Abuse Hoax' and was considered to be to be 'the sanest, most erudite, most professional and most accurate journalistic investigation into the satanic hysteria' to date in the USA. Although most American authorities have now discredited the allegations and consider it the result of social hysteria,

Stateside fundamentalists would simply not accept the verdict. So many US newspapers and magazines jumped on the bandwagon that when the incontrovertible evidence to prove otherwise reared its head, a press conspiracy reigned whereby reporting by the anti-occult newspapers never quite revealed the true extent of the facts, in order not to lose face. This in turn allowed the fundamentalists to continue their campaigns to prove their obsessions right.

The overall anti-occult campaign was not an isolated incident as one might first think - in fact, it is a tried and tested recipe, guaranteed to destroy the careers and lives of those who become embroiled in its slanders. The Mcmartin Pre-school trial was the event around which the original American version of satanic hysteria developed. The defendants, who were accused of hundreds of cases of child-abuse, torture, pornography and murder were acquitted - their lives utterly ruined - but within weeks, the carping hysteria of the mob had pressed for a re-investigation on undecided counts.

The investigation was based on the familiar testimony of a woman who had been hospitalised and diagnosed as paranoid schizophrenic, and who died from alcoholism before the trial ended. On her say so, the police mailed out a perjurative letter to several hundred parents whose children had at one time or another, attended the school and asked them to check for signs of sexual abuse.

Sexual abuse and mutilations had been carried out, according to child testimony, but there was no evidence to be found for any of the allegations. No pornographic photographs or equipment; no satanic regalia; no bodies could be produced. The bottom line was that you either believed the children or you didn't. To ensure that you did, fundamentalists and others began a "We believe the children" campaign and produced bumper stickers and slogan flags repeating the propaganda. It became a jingo of the day and not so strangely, perhaps, the N.S.P.C.C in the UK used a similar plea: "Childcare workers must believe the children, children just don't lie about this kind of thing ... you must listen to what the children are saying."

Independent medical investigations, however, proved that virtually all of the children who claimed to be abused in the Mcmartin case, had NOT been abused. Although one of them had actually been abused by his own father, not one of the defendants. The only evidence provided by the prosecution was derived from interviews by a private therapy group, which was commissioned by the police to investigate the allegations. The jury on the case roundly criticised this group and its approach. The children were badgered and questioned repetitively until they 'confessed' and most were questioned at least THIRTY times. One boy later admitted that he had said what his interviewer wanted him to say, just to escape.

None of the children's stories checked out. Some were impossible and involved helicopter flights and other fantasies. In response to one child claiming that there were tunnels underneath the building were the satanic rituals took place, the police dug up every square foot of ground but found nothing. By this time, hundreds of parents had formed themselves into a "We believe the children" group and insisted that the police had made a mistake. So they dug up the ground again and found nothing, although they dug deep enough to uncover Indian artefacts!

Despite the claims that thousands of children were involved in the satanic ceremonies, in an interview with *Green Egg Magazine*, San Francisco Police Inspector, Sandi Gallant replied that her personal feeling was that child abuse in America was not as extensive as the public were led to believe. Having worked on ritualistic crimes (even though they weren't titled as such) since 1978, she admitted that in her early days she was unable to differentiate between different belief systems and constantly confused the signs.

Considered to be one of the foremost authorities on 'ritualised crime' in the US, Ms Gallant now instructs fellow investigators on how to focus their attentions on the framework of ritualistic crime or abuse, rather than homing in on one particular religion. "Some one involved in a crime might use certain elements of a particular religious orientation to justify their crime, whether it's Christianity, Catholocism, Rastafarianism, Santeria, Satanism, or any combination of these things. You can't look at a room, see what looks like an upside-down star or an Ozzy Osbourne poster and say: 'This is a satanic crime'."

The Siege of the Sorcerer's Apprentice summarised the immense undercover growth of the anti-occult campaign that had built up in the UK, but the whole thing was not engineered overnight by a few fanatics. Plans to launch the campaign had been laid years before and since it was essential for the S.A.F.F to pin-point the exact area from where the attack was spearheaded, it directed all its administrative resources to uncovering and forcasting the development of the offensive.

The Mcmartin case clearly demonstrated how things occurred in the USA, giving the S.A.F.F the advantage of being able to predict with virtual certainty what was happening behind the scenes in the UK, by comparing Stateside experiences. Furthermore, they realised that the ritual-abuse scare was not the anti-occult campaign itself, but a symptom of it. Having seen similar cases to those in the States erupting in Nottingham, Cleveland and Rochdale, the belief that the UK would continue to suffer the backlash of anti-occultism, fuelled by Christian fundamentalism, was independently arrived at by *ORCRO Magazine.*

The intent behind the foundation of *ORCRO* in 1989 was non-trivial and twofold: to provide hard evidence where none had previously been cited as to the truth, or no, of the many allegations of child-abuse related to occultism, and to determine the source of the allegations.

Editor Peter Elliott outlined the aims and objectives of his publication: "The initial position of those associated with *ORCRO* was that the allegations made about occultism were the result of over enthusiastic amateurs letting their faith overbalance their capacity to reason and ask questions. Much of the Christian 'expert' comment as regard occultism indicated that they simply were not experts on occultism. That their material was, in many cases, second hand, inaccurate, misquoted and in general so full of holes that one could drive a bus through it! Court cases cited as examples of occult inspired crime, turned out, upon investigation, to be no such thing and promised court cases somehow never materialised - and continue not to materialise. Also much of the 'evidence' against occultism finally depended upon the Bible for its validity.

"In short, those persons most frequently quoted in the media, and who made the allegations against occultism, were considered to be an interesting aberration, worth looking into, but not to be regarded seriously. Without doubt many are sincere, but bright and well informed they are not, as the odd transcript penned by them shows. Lies about occultism emanating from Christians are nothing new. In general every religion misrepresents every other religion, but it is a different thing to move from the area of theological debate, to that of criminal accusation, and to set one's self up as judge, jury and executioner."

Independently, *ORCRO* then began to look into the American situation, working on the theory that events in the USA would to some degree reflect what subsequently happened in the UK - and what was going to happen. "When America sneezes, Europe catches the Black Death, etc. ..." Since most of the *ORCRO* team had business interests in the USA, they were able to build up an efficient and effective communications network with occult contacts in the States.

"What we discovered was not very nice." continued Peter Elliott. "In America the satanic child-abuse scare began in 1980 with the publication of a book describing a fictitious satanic ritual-sex scenario and to some degree culminated with the Mcmartin child-abuse trial. In the period between, many stories have emerged along with many 'anti-satanist' groups, many of whom will save your child - for a fee! It is very important to note that prior to the publication of that book, there is not one documented account of religiously organised and motivated child-abuse similar to the allegations now made by the 'anti-satanist' lobby. There are no 'satanic survivor' accounts prior to the publication of that book."

A further breakthrough came in Britain after S.A.F.F member Keith, put his Pagan beliefs on the line in a custody battle for his son. His wife, then a professed Pagan herself, had left him some time previously and at first did not claim custody of the boy. However when she later filed for custody, she cited Keith's beliefs as making him unsuitable to bring up the child. Well aware of the hype behind the anti-occult campaign, Keith fought a long, drawn out case using S.A.F.F library material to support the validity of his beliefs and, after hours of intensive questioning, Judge Wooley granted him custody of his son.

By the spring of 1991, exactly four years after the anti-occult campaign began, the tide began to ebb and *The Mail on Sunday* reported on the N.S.P.C.C's announcement that it was sorry for the 'wild statement about Satanism'. Back-tracking on its warnings of satanic sex rituals, the N.S.P.C.C admitted there was not 'a shred of evidence' to support its claims made in a two-year national investigation. A spokesman said that the N.S.P.C.C had launched its warning against devil-worshippers in 1989 as the result of a survey among its national team members and justified the action because ...

" ... many of the team members involved are very experienced ... I believe we were right to be concerned".

For the reason as to why respectable bodies were caught up in the satanic hysteria, S.A.F.F organisers believe that the Social Services and child-welfare charities ran out of steam with their campaign about incest in families, and that their enthusiasm and euphoria died a death when the problem (and it IS obviously a serious problem) turned out not to be as widespread and horrendous as originally estimated by media hype. The S.A.F.F contend that the 'professions' jumped on the bandwagon of 'satanic child-abuse' in an unwritten conspiracy to vindicate themselves and reaffirm their *raison d'etre* within society. They did this, not because they had any proof but because they thought it an unquestionably good thing to do, since the campaign brought *cross-cultural support* and added new impetus to social work.

Into this seething maelstrom of lies and distortion, Christian fundamentalists had stirred the grim spectre of child-murder and abuse. Regular interviews with leading figures in the anti-occult campaign quickly identified the principle antagonists but it took four years before the media finally got around to 'nailing the lies of the satanic abuse industry' as *The Mail of Sunday* so aptly described it. Finally hoisted on their own petard, one by one the anti-occult campaigners were 'nailed' by the very media on whom they had perpetrated one of the cruelest hoaxes of the 20th century.

No doubt anti-occult campaigners and the media were working on the principle that if a number of monkeys were allowed to bash away on several typewriters for an unspecified period of time, they would eventually produce a poem; trawl in enough suspected child-abuse cases and one will eventually prove to have satanic/occult connections. This proved, however, not to be the case. In the whole of the five year campaign NOT ONE case of occult-abuse linked crime was brought to court.

All that the S.A.F.F prophesied came to pass as the furore surrounding the satanic myth was quashed by court rulings. The repercussions, however, linger on. The outbursts in Parliament, which started the myth in the first place were untrue and inaccurate. There were NO Witches in league with the Devil, actively working against Christianity and sexually molesting children in their rites. Only in the minds of the deluded were babies produced to be sacrificed to the Devil and throughout the entire anti-occult campaign it was not the occult community who showed itself to be feeble-willed.

The alleged information was never sent to the Home Office and although no occultists were prosecuted for child-abuse during the five year period, *a large number of the clergy were.* The S.A.F.F's bulging 'Naughty Vicar File' illustrates that despite the fact that this aspect of ritualised abuse is recognised as a problem by social workers, those in the profession have turned a blind eye to this *identifiable* threat in favour of chasing the Devil! It is also incongruous that *The Church Times* (issue 6631) chose to feature an article entitled 'Increase in Ritual Abuse of Children Combated by Clergy', when one of the country's foremost experts in child-abuse is on record as saying in an interview: "I have worked with more vicars who have abused than ever Satan worshippers."

The increasing weakness of orthodox Christianity in the UK blinkered the vision of the clergy to the dangers of fundamentalism, although many of them were quick enough to condemn Islamic fundamentalism when it manifested itself during the Salman Rushdie affair and the Gulf War. Author Michael Howard believes that the failure of orthodox religion to provide spiritual sustenance for the newly educated class resulted in this tremendous revival of interest in the occult sciences. The New Age movement, so loathed by the anti-occultists, embraces both Eastern and Western forms of belief, in an attempt to offer the individual the opportunity to communicate with his own god without the interference of a 'priestly middle man'.

But even if people are suspicious of the occult revival, not all New Age thinking can be bad. "One of the most important aspects of the movement" writes Howard, "is that it embraces such varied subjects as ecology and 'green'politics, alternative medicine, hi-tech science, Eastern religion, quantum physics and feminism in an attempt to look at society in a unified way ... The sooner the subversive activities of the fundamentalists can be curbed, the sooner mankind will find a common understanding and tolerance of alternative religion, science and art."

Chapter 12: The Counter Offensive

ertainly no treatise on Satanism and Witchcraft would be complete without mention of demoniacal or hysterical possession, for it was on charges such as these that hundreds of innocent parties were accused of Witchcraft and died at the stake or end of a rope. Modern psychology now seems convinced that the majority of those purporting to be bewitched or possessed were in fact, suffering from certain forms of mental illness and/or sexual repression.

It has even been suggested that the attitudes of society of the times fostered and encouraged the forms of exhibitionism and hysterical manifestations. We must remember that the worst of the Witch-hunts carried out in Britain came at a time when puritan morality was on the upsurge, when academic learning was on the increase and the boundaries of the world rapidly expanding. English history cannot escape totally with the excuse of medieval superstition and ignorance.

In many parts of the world, many religious sects (including a few of Christian ones) encourage possession as part of their regular mode of worship, believing that the members of the congregation, reduced to writhing and gibbering on the floor, are speaking with holy tongues. The study of possession is, in itself, a fascinating subject and there is not room enough in this book to fully examine the phenomena but there are numerous recorded cases whereby those accused of Witchcraft were held to be responsible for inducing possession.

Instead of permitting random members of the clergy to dabble in exorcism or deliverance ministry, it would be more fitting for the Church to issue copies of Marc Cramer's *The Devil Within*, which was: "The first in-depth psychological and parapsychological study of possession in terms of the darkest depths of the unconscious mind." If Cramer's book were to be taken seriously by historian and Church alike it would be necessary to re-write the whole sordid history of Salem, Loudun and the Witches of Warboys - and admit that most of those concerned were ***murdered*** on the evidence of self-induced hysteria in the children who acted as their accusers.

The most frightening aspect of current Church involvement in deliverance ministry, however, raises the question of whether the majority of those carrying out exorcisms are qualified to diagnose and identify what may possibly be serious psychiatric disorders. Studies have shown that the hysterical excitement connected with possession is highly contagious and can rapidly transmit itself from one person to a group within a very short period of time. Modern psychiatric investigations recognise that possession is indeed a mental condition and that current misreading of symptoms and causes have led to the deaths (mainly by suicide) of the victims.

One of the most notorious examples of possession is the infamous episode of the Salem Witches which clearly documents how a whole township was torn apart by fear, malice and blind prejudice. It began just after Christmas 1691, when the nine-year old daughter of the Rev. Samuel Parris and her eleven-year old cousin began exhibiting strange symptoms of what later became described as possession; and culminated in the hanging of nineteen people, one 80-year old man 'pressed' to death and hundreds more imprisoned.

A hot-bed of New England puritanism, Salem Village was constantly engaged in a vendetta with neighbours over some real or imagined insult. A contemporary account states that: "It is little wonder, then, that even in a colony renowned for the litigiousness and obstinacy of its inhabitants, Salem Village should have become something of a byword for stiff-necked quarrelsome confrontations ... This, then, was the place of argument, aggravation and aggression over which the Rev. Samual Parris, himself an obstinate, self-righteous and tactless man who had failed as a merchant in Barbados, ministered on the eve of the Witchcraft crisis."

It transpired that the girls had been dabbling with fortune-telling and implicated the household slaves, Tituba and John Indian. "It has usually been assumed that this (couple) were West Indians, assets from their master's otherwise disastrous Caribbean ventures. They may, however, have been 'Red Indians'; whatever their origins, they were tainted with heathenism and devil-worship, especially Tituba who claimed that her mother had been a witch."

As the Folio contemporary account, *The Witches of Salem*, observes: "Those (initially) accused by the girls were from the most vulnerable, least respectable stratum of society. All were women; one was not only a slave but also recently arrived in the community and perhaps exotic. Good was an habitual scrounger and Osborne's reputation had been clouded by her living with a man who she only later married."

Thrown into prison, the terrified Tituba gave evidence that transformed the 'apparently conventional charge against a couple of despised women' into a sulphur impregnated satanic plot; her account of covenants, familiars, flights and spectres plunged Salem into a medieval world of supernatural fear and vengeance.

The pressure that was brought to bear on the ignorant slave-woman only came out later when she revealed that she had been beaten and abused by Parris in order to make her confess. In addition he refused to pay her [prison] fees unless she stood by her confession. "If Parris withheld her prison fees, she would come near to both freezing and starving and could not be released."

Over two hundred people, many of them respectable, were subsequently implicated in the allegations and, as a result, several of them were hanged while their neighbours look on. As to the question of why such infamy was able to happen, there have been an assortment of answers:

Sexual frustrations induced by puritan repression;
A revolt by daughters against their mothers, psychologically
displaced on to other women of their mother's generation;
Chadwick Hanson's diagnosis of 'genuine clinical hysteria,
with its extraordinary psychosomatic symptoms and suggestibility induced by adolescent guilt-feelings';
Or a just girlish hoax which got completely out of hand?

Whatever the reasons, *Man, Myth & Magic* records that: "There was a public revulsion of feeling during the later trials, none of the later suspects were punished, and a heated controversy broke out on whether there ever had been any Witchcraft in the community at all, or whether the whole affair had been a tragic delusion ... Colonial America never again dared to carry out the death sentence for Witchcraft."

Loudun, in France, was described by Aldous Huxley *(The Devils of Loudun)* as a large but thinly-populated, inward-looking provincial town and an important Protestant stronghold in which the power of the Catholics had reasserted itself. "Into this antagonism, in 1617, strode Urbain Grandier, intelligent, educated by the Jesuits and appointed by them to two benefices in the town, an excellent preacher, attractive, outspoken and proud."

Despite his calling, he had an eye for young women and, although not uncommon in priests in 17th century France, his lack of discretion, and his 'unguarded tongue' made him many enemies. Having carried on a scandalous affair with one of his young penitents, and accused of impregnating the daughter of the public prosecutor, Grandier found himself arrested, charged with immorality and found guilty. Nevertheless, having friends in high places, he was freed and returned to Loudun to resume his clerical duties - but there was more trouble in store.

Outside gossip about Grandier's affairs had no doubt leaked into the neighbouring Ursuline convent and reached the ears of the Mother Superior, Sister Jeanne des Anges, who promptly developed the 'hots' for the hapless priest. Grandier was the epitome of the forbidden pleasures of the flesh and upon his refusal to accept the appointment of confessor to the convent, the unattractive, middle-aged prioress aligned herself with his enemies. Soon after, the Mother Superior and several other nuns began to give 'bizarre signs of demonic possession by going into convulsions, adopting erotic postures, holding their breaths and distorting their faces and voices'.

Grandier's name began to be mentioned and before long he was arrested on charges of bewitching the nuns, tortured and burnt alive at the stake. According to most accounts, there is no doubt, even amongst Roman Catholic authorities, that Urbain Grandier was innocent of the charges brought against him. To the embarrassment of the clergy, the possession continued long after Grandier was gone. Jeanne des Anges, the true villain of the piece, it appears had 'discovered the art of shamming sanctity, claimed to experience visions and generally counterfeited an image of saintliness' long before her appointment at Loudun! Heresy hast no fury like a woman scorned.

The Warboys incident, however, was possibly one of the most

important Witch-trials in England, after which Alice Samuals, her husband and daughter were executed as Witches after the five adolescent daughters of the local Squire had accused the Samuals family of bewitching them. Despite the local doctor hinting at Witchcraft after treating the girls for a sudden attack of 'fits', the parents initially acted quite sensibly and dismissed the whole thing as 'childish wantoness'. However, as the symptoms increased, they were forced to confront a respectable and elderly neighbour with their daughters' accusations. The fits became more and more frequent and the whole episode may have eventually have sorted itself out had it not been for the interference of a certain Lady Cromwell - grandmother of that puritan extremist, Oliver.

Lady Cromwell physically attacked the old lady, acting on the belief that if you draw blood above a Witches' breath, then her spell would be broken. Mrs Samuals, it is reported, asked why she was being used in such a manner, adding: "I never did you any harm as yet". When Lady Cromwell died two years later, the ominously sounding 'yet' was emphasised and used as evidence that Mrs Samuals was responsible for Lady Cromwell's death by magic.

The neighbourhood got the wind up; the Throckmorton girls were still giving award winning performances and so the Samuals family were brought before the Bishop of Lincoln for examination. All three were found guilty and hanged. Agnes Samuals refused to confess and declined to 'plead her belly' (pregnancy being the recognised and permissible escape), by retorting that it would never be said of her that she was a whore as well as a Witch!

Like Salem and Loudun, the Warboys case is important because it involved people of respectability, education and influence and was widely reported in contemporary publications. The repressed hysteria and self-induced symptoms of adolescence (or frustration), were laid at the door of those unfortunates destined for the fire or hangman's noose. Even today, courtesy of film and fiction, the myth of demoniacal possession is perpetuated.

Many of the dénouements cannot be excused by mental or sexual fantasy but probably have their foundations in sheer malice. Young boys and girls pointed the finger of accusation at all manner of folk and in Pendle in 1634 a young lad must have thought he was onto a winner when he falsely accused a number of local people. Amongst them was a certain Janet Device who was herself the daughter of a convicted Witch and who, as a child, had been responsible for her own mother's execution. The boy later retracted his statement but not before three of the accused (but not the unsinkable Janet) had died in prison.

English juries were rightly nervous over such testimonies but this did not prevent two respectable women from being executed in Bury in 1644 on a child's destructive evidence. One case came to light in 1620 involving a lad who claimed to be bewitched and urinated a blue liquid. *(Man, Myth & Magic)* This was caused by stuffing ink-soaked paper under his foreskin and pouring a generous measure of ink into the chamber pot! In this instance the boy was made to apologise to his victim but there were whisperings that the lad had been coached by a Catholic priest, which compounds the malice.

Marc Cramer holds a MA in Psychology and is a leading authority on parapsychological issues, as well as a member of the Society for Psychical Research and his book was the result of extensive study and research into the subject, as well as first hand witnessing of possession. Cramer reached three fundamental conclusions: Firstly that the 'overwhelming majority' of all reported cases of possession have been induced by hysteria or are outright frauds, and that ***true demoniacal possession is exceedingly rare.***

While he believes that the existence of manifestations of possession are something distinct from 'mythomania' or madness, it does not follow through that the possession is actually caused by evil spirits or demons. Cramer also explains that while there is every reason to believe that so-called demon infestation is a psychological (but not supernatural) event, the syndrome is not directly related to other mental disorders and belongs to a different category.

Not all cases of possession are the province of disordered minds or the rare instance of genuine demonic possession. The dreaded affliction of St. Anthony's Fire broke out in scores of medieval towns and villages affecting whole communities. Causing the 'flesh to burn like the fires of hell' by constricting the blood vessels, as well as producing hallucinations and peculiar actions in the victims, the medieval peasant truly believed that he was beset by demons. In modern times the disease has been identified as ergot poisoning, caused by a fungus on rye flour kept too long over winter.

Similarly the curses and spells that were claimed to be responsible for the illnesses and accidents afflicting the neighbourhood can, in modern times, be shown to stem from the mind. Lyall Watson in *Supernature* maintains that at least half of all the ills of mankind can be diagnosed as originating in the mind.

If it is possible to exert conscious control over unconscious processes, then the reverse is also bound to occur. It shows up in fact in all the psychosomatic disorders that surround us today. Watson cites tribal witch-doctors who always treat all diseases by magic as well as by herbal cures, and their success rate with skin complaints, blood-pressure difficulties, peptic ulcer, incipient coronary thrombosis and hysterical blindness is as high, if not higher, than that of specially trained Harley Street specialists.

Watson also claims that even accidental injuries, such as broken limbs, can often be attributed to psychological causes; recent research shows that the statement "It happened by accident" and "It happened by chance" are not synonymous. Some people at certain times really are accident prone. Personality traits, psychological conditions and even physiological patterns can be identified in individuals who are nothing more than 'accidents looking for a place to happen'.

"Taken to its limit, autosuggestion can even kill," he continues. "Every year thousands of people die simply because they believe that it is inevitable. **Witchcraft may have powers that are truly supernatural, but it does not need them while people are capable of wishing themselves to death.** It is not necessary to consciously believe in forces of evil; the unconscious can manage very well on its own."

And a final instance of modern medical discovery dispels a further facet of the Witch-myth concerning the aged crones who were the obvious targets for branding as Witches. This is the onset of failing faculties, senile dementia, and in some cases, paraphrenia (a type of schizophrenia found in the aged), that are all characteristics of old age. The mutterings, quarrelsomeness and strange habits of one thus inflicted, would closely resemble surviving accounts of evidence of Witch-behaviour and if modern thinking can rid itself of a belief in curses and pacts with the Devil, it would rid itself of a lot of superstitious nonsense that still surrounds the Craft.

Much of the evidence against Satanism comes from the bogus survivor accounts but as Anton Lavey points out in his biography: "... there's a centre for multiple personalities studying 'adult survivors of satanic child abuse'. Now what's that supposed to mean? There was no modern, organised satanic movement before I came along, and here are all these middle-aged women telling how they were raped and tortured as children, when their parents belonged to a satanic cult? That would have been in the 1940's. There were none! Lord knows, I looked. Producers don't send camera crews out to tracks down these women's parents and get *their* stories; no one looks up the women's psychological histories ..."

Multiple Personality Disorder has replaced possession in modern clinical parlance but the doctrine is not fully understood or accepted in the U.K. According to S.A.F.F guidelines, the basic idea seems to be that consciousness represses trauma from memory by locking away that part of the 'personality' which was foremost at the time of suffering. The only way it can be released artificially (we are told), is through the process of hypnotic regression which 'unlocks' that aspect of the personality and 'reminds' the consciousness of what happened. But it added its own warning: "We are not saying that people who relate abuse during regression have not been abused, we are saying that the circumstances of such abuse may easily be *contaminated by the mechanics of the mind*, and that too many therapists self-seek their own preconceptions with regard to allegations of ritual abuse during regression with MPD victims."

Looking at the problem from another angle, other doctors have come up with False Memory Syndrome, which they claim is an alarming new phenomenon in which vulnerable adults, encouraged by over-enthusiastic therapists, 'remember' abuse that never took place. Journalist Anthea Gerrie, investigated FMS in her article 'The Accused' in *Options* magazine and reported that: "When a suggestible patient encounters a therapist who believes most children have been sexually abused in childhood, hysteria can break out - especially in group sessions where women may try to outdo each other with their sensational 'memories'. Torture, murder, Satanism and even cannibalism figure in many 'memories' aired in these groups".

Even accounting for medical disorders that contributed to satanic hysteria in America and the U.K, it does not explain the superstitious polemics behind the ferocity of 20th century fundamentalist campaigning against those of a different belief. In his book *The Human Zoo*, Desmond Morris took a brutally objective look at the society the human animal has created for itself, and the reasoning behind the reaction to differing cultural influences and backgrounds being perceived as a threat.

Morris poses the question: What is the difference between black natives slicing up a white missionary, and a white mob lynching a helpless Negro? The answer is very little. Whatever the reasons or excuses, the basic behaviour mechanism is the same. They are both cases of members of the in-group attacking members of the out-group.

This is an area, Morris's explanation continues, where it is difficult to maintain our objectivity for we are, each one of us, a member of some particular in-group, and it is difficult for us to view the problems of inter-group conflict without, however unconsciously, taking sides. Unless members of the in-group have personal interchange and knowledge of the out-group as individuals, the inter-group hostility will harden and the out-group will feel the need to band together for defence. Less and less contact will take place between members of the two groups and before long, they will be acting as if they belonged to two different tribes. It is not possible to force peoples of different cultures/beliefs into understanding; likewise, it is never possible to decree or legislate faith out of existence.

Understanding appears to be the basic key-word missing from the majority of occult/fundamentalist exchanges but although newspaper and magazine editors are beginning to use bland, innocuous articles on the occult, these are still frowned on by many because they represent the Craft in a nebulous light.

Miriem Clay Egerton is quick to criticise those 'media Witches' whom, she says: "Appear giving their impression that they are armed with a yardbrush and a never emptying cauldron of whitewash for the Craft. As a Witch I rather object to having such an apologetic attitude taken on behalf of the Craft. Why are they always bleating? Why always simpering that we are misunderstood; that the Craft is pure in its goodness and lack of harm?

"It is a religion of life and of nature - and life and nature are not a bed of roses without thorns. In nature creatures die. Not by gracefully sinking into a peaceful sleep but far more frequently of hunger when too old to hunt, or at the teeth and claws of predators -

predators given life and purpose by the God and Goddess. The God and Goddess are not do-gooder social workers living in Surrey, and viewing the world through rose tinted spectacles! The Lord of Life is also the Lord of Death; the Maiden is also the Morrigham. If 'modern' wet-behind-the-ears, eco-obsessed neo-Pagans wish to proclaim a belief in living an unnatural kiddies fairy story, more power to their imagination, but please don't try to make the general public, or newcomers, think that this is all there is to the Craft."

Conversely, Anton Lavey believes that the adverse publicity has done Satanism no harm. "When satanic hysteria gets to the point of absurdity, people start questioning the whole line of crap. It will eventually get so that no one believes anything the Christian ministers say anymore. When (people) hear about the Devil and how rotten he is, it just makes them curious about what the Satanic viewpoint might be."

And as Blanche Barton points out, there are already those questioning the wild claims, since the accusers can produce no hard evidence to support their allegations. She sites the 1989 report by the Committee for the Scientific Examination of Religion on the claims of various 'breeders' and satanic survivors. After a thorough investigation, the report concluded that: "The most shocking claims, those involving the abductions and ritual murder of children, are easily shown to be false. The allegations of large scale Satanic conspiracies are totally without foundation. In fact, the available evidence leaves only one reasonable conclusion: *they do not exist!*" [Their italics.]

Since the Middle Ages the majority of charges levelled against occultism have been founded on sexual activities of one form or another. As William Sargant points out in *Man, Myth & Magic*, the words 'venerate' and 'venereal' are etymologically connected, stemming from the Latin goddess of love, Venus. Amongst pre-Christian cultures, sex played an intrinsic role 'in religion, magic, mysticism, occultism, symbolism and the whole range of human dealings with the supernatural'. It was the advent of Papal control in Europe that decreed that sex for anything other than procreation was the province of the Devil. The physiological act of sex and orgasm greatly increases suggestibility, according to Sargant, which may then fire off further sexual excitement with repeatedly induced orgasmic collapse producing states of deep hysterical trance.

It was by similar recorded means that Aleister Crowley obtained an altered state of consciousness when he conducted a series of magical experiments using sexual means: "On the appointed day he is attended by one or more experienced attendants whose duty it is to exhaust him sexually by every known means. The candidate will sink into a sleep of utter exhaustion but he must again sexually stimulated and then again allowed to fall asleep. This alternation is to continue indefinitely until the candidate is in a state which is neither sleep, nor waking, and in which his spirit is set free by perfect exhaustion of the body ... (and) communes with the most Highest and the Most Holy Lord God of its Being, Maker of Heaven and Earth."

Although, as we have seen in a previous chapter, there are elements of sex magic in most aspects of Craft-lore, much of the theory and practice of sex magic has been introduced into the West from Eastern cultures. Not all practitioners have such lofty ideals and sex magic can also used for more down to earth purposes. According to Sargant, by focusing his Will on the desired object of the operation, a magician generates powerful physical and psychological energy with which he is able to influence people and events around him. "In magical theory a sexual working has no hope of success if the magician allows himself to be swept away in the thundering surf of desire and orgasm," continues Sargant. "Unless he remains the master of the force he has aroused, he cannot divert it at his objective. In general in religious and magical sexual rites the element of pleasure is secondary; it is the means to the goal, not the goal itself."

Powerful social and religious taboos still surround sex outside marriage, particularly in Christian, Judaic and Islamic cultures where sexual pleasure is considered to be inherently sinful and demonic; and the strong emphasis which Christians, in particular, have placed upon virginity and celibacy, have left their indelible mark on Western attitudes. For this reason alone, it is unlikely that the (predominantly Christian) in-group would be willing to take steps to understand what they consider to be a highly immoral (minority occult/Pagan) out-group.

The highly potent image of Witchcraft and Satanism firmly entrenched in public and media minds is aptly illustrated by the story of a journalist and his wife who decided to investigate 'the powers of darkness' for a Sunday sleaze. The couple let it be known around certain clubs and public houses in London that they were interested in black magic and before long, they were approached and invited attend a black mass - for a fee of twenty pounds! The ceremony turned out to be a 'rather badly staged obscene exhibition' which rather disappointed the couple.

Nevertheless our intrepid journalist persevered until he was convinced he was onto the real thing when he stumbled across evidence of an 'occult set-up' in a derelict farmhouse, consisting of burnt out black candles in a double circle, evidence of incense, bloody feathers and a charred Bible. His photographs of the scene were published in the Sunday tabloid and as a result, the couple were approached and invited to participate in further rituals - for a total fee (including disbursements) of almost £100.

According to his article published some time later, the couple returned on several occasions to witness the *usual* nude scenarios of sacrificial black cockerels, naked acolytes, ritual ravishment and spell casting. They apparently decided to bow out when they learned that they were next on the menu for ritual sex with the leader of the group as part of their 'confirmation' ceremony. Needless to say there was the *usual* catalogue of recriminations but although the journalist subsequently condemned all serious involvement in black magic, his fascination with the occult remained to the extent that he constructed an enormous pentacle on the lawn of his home - no doubt to impress or frighten the neighbours.

If the naive go around pubs and clubs advertising their willingness to participate in 'black magic' ceremonies, one can only suggest that they reaped exactly what they had sown, if indeed their story be true. They were willing to adopt a voyeuristic approach to ritual rape and animal sacrifice - and pay for the privilege. The injured tone of the narrative evokes little sympathy from the reader, and one assumes our journalist was well paid by his tabloid masters for his pains.

A similar experience befell a young man who joined an amateur theatre group run by a charismatic director with highly compelling intellectual and sexual qualities. The young actor was subsequently invited to participate in a bizarre ceremony of group sex liberally laced with satanic overtones and as a result suffered from appalling nightmares and hallucinations. After weeks of mental and physical torment he began to believe that he was indeed possessed. After near-disaster with a group of Evangelicals, the youth finally confided in a sensible and sympathetic priest who made him realise that he'd been *under the psychological domination of the theatre director, not the Devil!*

The impressionable actor was quoted as saying: "I believe in the power of evil, I've experienced it and it's terrible; and I believe that I've been helped by Christianity; but I don't believe in demons and all that stuff. The sort of thing I experienced is much more frightening than any demon."

Mind control is not a 20th century phenomena; having consumed a lethal cocktail of drink, drugs and (sometimes unlawful) sex, the unsuspecting can be drawn into a whirlpool of deception and complicity so aptly described by Rollo Ahmed in the opening chapter. Such groups do exist. The S.A.F.F knows they exist *but none are genuine occultists.* Similar to the old Hell Fire Club, they exist only for the gratification of the flesh and control over others, but without the intellectual expression of Sir Francis Dashwood and his 'brothers'.

The problem lies in the fact that in operating under the guise of satanic ceremony, reality becomes blurred, resulting in establishment, religious and media bodies being unable to distinguish between genuine Witchcraft/Satanism and duplicity. During the initial outbreak of satanic hysteria Chris Bray offered publicly to pool the resources of the S.A.F.F to combat the real problems of growing paedophilia and bogus occultism, but his entreaties were ignored, simply because he was tagged with the blanket 'satanic' label that persistently confuses issues surrounding the occult.

Similarly, many occultists do not believe there has really been an anti-occult conspiracy at all, or that the detrimental behaviour of a small number of outsiders, threatens the whole structure of occultism/Paganism. Chris Bray experienced great difficulties in activating the community five years ago when he first saw the spectre of satanic hysteria manifesting itself in journalistic and Evangelical quarters. His problem was that none of the influential members of the community would listen; they insisted that it was all another seven-day wonder and, according to the organiser of the S.A.F.F, some of them are still insisting that.

Even though the first major battle has been won and the fundamentalist anti-occult scare with its attendant satanic hysteria and ritualistic child-abuse allegations have been totally discredited, the war is far from over. S.A.F.F intelligence knows that the fundamentalists are regrouping, changing tactics and altering their image - but, insists Chris Bray, the REAL dangers are still to come.

In conclusion

o relate the whole complex story surrounding the five year anti-occult campaign would take several volumes devoted to that subject alone. However, for those who seriously wish to discover more about the phenomena of satanic hysteria, the S.A.F.F. archive and library holds thousands of newspaper and magazine clippings chronicling its development from 1988. The S.A.F.F has also published dozens of guidelines and pamphlets on various important aspects of the anti-occult campaign.

Much of this information is now accessible to researchers and details of specific events or interests can be obtained by sending a self-addressed envelope with first class postage or International Reply Coupons to The S.A.F.F., 6/8 Burley Lodge Road, Leeds LS6 1QP, Yorkshire, U.K..

APPENDIX I

THE PAGAN CREDO*

Compiled by Stewart & Janet Farrar with help from Leonora James, Chris Bray and other Pagans.

1. Paganism is a religion (or field of related religions) in its own right, being traceable from prehistoric times through most ancient and modern cultures, and making a continuing contribution to the spiritual evolution of our species.

2. It is not rigid or dogmatic in form; its exact expression depends on the individual Pagan, or willingly co-operating group of Pagans. This Credo is therefore itself not dogma, but an attempt to describe the mainstream characteristics of Pagan philosophy.

3. Paganism aims to offer a way to recognise and attune oneself with the manifold forces of Nature, which already exist within and without us, and which are vital to our survival, fulfilment and evolution. By celebrating the seasons and becoming one with other living creatures, Pagans synchronise intimately with the planet, and liberate their personalities and magnify their perceptions and talents, in the interests of themselves, their groups and communities, and humankind as a whole.

4. Paganism believes in the same Divine Creative Force as anyone else, because if there is one there can only be One. Like any other religion, Paganism personifies this Ultimate as a means of attuning oneself to it, because it cannot be apprehended directly, except perhaps in brief flashes of intuition.

5. Paganism's basic personification of the Ultimate is in its creative polarisation of male and female aspects, as the Father God and the Mother Goddess. The God represents the fertilising, energising, analysing, intellectual, left-brain-function aspects. The Goddess represents the formative, nourishing, synthesising, intuitive, right-brain-function aspects.

6. As above, so below; this basic Divine polarisation is the primal cause of all manifestation, and it is reflected at all levels of being, including ourselves.

7. Pagans make use of many different God- and Goddess-forms as tuning-signals to different aspects of the essential God and Goddess. These forms vary according to cultural, geographical and personal backgrounds, and are USUALLY (and naturally, since men and women aspire to emulate them) envisaged in perfected human form; but they are all valid. They are real, in the same sense that if one attunes oneself to them sincerely, they are vitalised and empowered by the Ultimate of which they represent aspects. They are not idols, but are the numinous archetypal symbols which are vital (or in everyday language, 'God-given') components of the human Collective Unconscious.

8. Pagans do not worship the Devil; that would be totally incompatible with the principle of paragraphs 4 and 7 above. The Devil of monotheist religions does not exist in Pagan philosophy; Pagans regard evil as an imbalance to be corrected, not as an independent force or entity.

9. Like all religions, Paganism believes in multi-level reality. These levels are generally defined in Pagan thinking as the spiritual, mental, astral, etheric and physical levels. Each level has its own laws, but the laws of different levels do not conflict with each other.

10. Pagans regard all these levels as equally holy, and essential parts of the cosmic spectrum of manifestation. They totally reject the Dualistic concept which equates the spiritual with good and matter with evil.

11. Pagan philosophy and worship therefore tend to be strongly Nature-based. Mother Earth is not a temporary stopping-place, but our home, of which we are a living part, and for the health and protection of which we bear a constant responsibility.

12. The Pagan view of the Cosmos is essentially organic. The Ultimate is its creative life-force; but all manifestation is part of the total organism. Our own Planet can be regarded as one limb or organ of it, and we ourselves (and all Earth's other creatures and components) as cells within that limb or organ. Our health depends on its health, and vice versa.

13. Paganism therefore does not envisage a gulf between Creator and Created. The spectrum is continuous and interdependent. Each individual is of the same nature as the Source, and is capable of being a channel for it.

14. On the basis of the foregoing, most Pagans regard all sincere religions as different paths to the same truths. The particular Deity-personification, symbology, and meaningful mythology which suit one person as tuning-signals to the Ultimate may not suit another. Pagans are therefore essentially ecumenical, non-proselytising, and tolerant.

15. This does not mean that Pagans cannot voice constructive criticism of the attitudes of some religious hierarchies, or of the narrowness and bigotry of some dogmatic systems. Pagans reject as dangerous and destructive, in particular, the belief that one's own religion is the only true one, and that all others are devilish and therefore to be condemned and persecuted.

16. Pagans lay more emphasis on continuing spiritual development than on instant revelation, though they accept that the latter can sometimes happen - usually as a breakthrough to consciousness of a longer unconscious accumulation.

17. Most Pagans believe in reincarnation, in one form or another. This belief further strengthens Pagans' attitude to Earth as our continuing home for the foreseeable future, rather than a temporary and restrictive stopping-place. It is also a powerful moral force, because it emphasises that all offences against other individuals, the community, or the Earth, and all failure to learn lessons, must ultimately be put right by oneself, and cannot be evaded by bodily death.

18. Pagans' ethical attitude is often summed up in the sentence: "An it harm none, do what you will." This means achieving full self-development while accepting equally full responsibility towards one's fellow-humans, one's fellow-creatures, and the Earth itself. Love for all of these is the foundation-stone of Paganism. In particular, Pagans feel a special responsibility towards the young; their vulnerability must not be abused, and they must be helped to develop themselves according to their own natures, so that when they are mature they can chose their own paths - and their own religious forms - with maximum awareness and without pressurisation from their elders.

* The above text has been reproduced in its original 1989 edition although it has been published in some magazines under the title 'Pagan Beliefs'.

APPENDIX II

The Nine Satanic Statements

1. Satan represents indulgence, instead of abstinence!
2. Satan represents vital existence, instead of spiritual pipe-dreams!
3. Satan represents undefiled wisdom, instead of hypocritical self-deceit!
4. Satan represents kindness to those who deserve it, instead of love wasted on ingrates!
5. Satan represents vengeance, instead of turning the other cheek!
6. Satan represents responsibilities to the responsible, instead of concern for psychic vampires!
7. Satan represents man as just another animal, sometimes better, more often worse than those that walk on all-fours, who, because of his "divine spiritual and intellectual development", has become the most vicious animal of all!
8. Satan represents all of the so-called sins, as they all lead to physical, mental, or emotional gratification!
9. Satan has been the best friend the church has ever hand, as he has kept it in business all these years!

The Eleven Satanic Rules of the Earth

1. Do not give opinions or advice unless you are asked.
2. Do not tell your troubles to others unless you are sure that they want to hear them.
3. When in another's lair, show him respect or else do not go there.
4. If a guest in your lair annoys you, treat him cruelly and without mercy.
5. Do not make sexual advances unless you are given the mating signal.
6. Do not take that which does not belong to you unless it is a burden to the other person and he cries out to be relieved.
7. Acknowledge the power of magic if you have employed it successfully to obtain your desires. If you deny the power of magic, you will lose all you have obtained.
8. Do not complain about anything to which you need not subject yourself.
9. Do not harm little children.
10. Do not kill non-human animals unless attacked or for your food.
11. When walking in open territory, bother no one. If someone bothers you, ask him to stop. If he does not stop, destroy him.

APPENDIX III

An extract from *The Masque of Queens* by Ben Jonson

Possibly to demonstrate the depth of his classical learning, Jonson's richly annotated version of *The Masque of Queens* freely acknowledges that he had drawn heavily on classical literature for the activities of his characters. " ... all the power attributed to Witches by the ancients ... Homer to Circe in the *Odyssey*. Theocritus to Simatha in *Idyll II, The Sorceress*. Virgil to Alphesiboes in his *Eight Eclogue*. Ovid to Dipses in his *Amores*, to Medea and Circe in the *Metamorphoses*. Tibulles to Saga. Horace to Canidia, Sagana, Veiga and Folia. Seneca to Medea and the Nurse in *Hercules on Oeta*. Petronius Arbiter to his Saga in the fragment known as *Satyricon*, and Claudian to his Megaera in book one of his poem *On Rufinus*, who takes the habit of a Witch ..."

No doubt compiled from additional common gossip of the time, the following provides the centre piece for the anti-Masque before the Witches, ie. evil, are put to flight by 'heroic virtue'. In 1978 part was set to music by the Lancashire based folkgroup, *Strawhead*.

I have been all day looking after
A raven, feeding on a quarter;
And soon as she turned her beak to the south,
I snatched this morsel out of her mouth.

I have been gathering wolves hairs,
The mad dog's foam and the adder's ear,
The spurging of a dead man's eyes,
And all since the evening star die rise.

I last night lay all alone
One the ground, to hear the Mandrake groan,
And plucked him up, though he grew full low,
As as I had done, the cock did crow.

And I have been choosing out this skull
From Charnel-houses that were full,
From private grots, and public pits,
And frightened the sexton out of his wits.

Under the cradle I did creep
By day, and when the child was asleep,
At night I sucked the breath; and rose,
And plucked the nodding nurse by the nose.

I had a dagger, what did I with that?
Killed an infant to have his fat.
A piper it got, at the church-ale,
I bade him again blow wind in the tail.

A murderer yonder was hung in chains,
The sun and the wind had shrunk his veins;
I bit off a sinew, I chipped his hair,
I brought off his rags that danced in the air.

The screech-owl's eggs and the feathers black,
The blood of a frog and the bone in his back,
I have been getting, and made of his skin
A purset, to keep Sir Cranion in.

And I have been plucking, plants among,
Hemlock, henbane, adder's tongue,
Nightshade, moonwort, leopard's bane,
and twice by the dogs was like to be ta'en.

I from the jaws of the gardener's bitch
Did snatch these bones, and then leaped the ditch,
Yet went I back to the house again,
Killed the black cat - and here's the brain.

I went to the toad breeds under the wall,
I charmed him out, and he came at my call
I scratched out the eyes of the owl, before:
I tore the bat's wing; what would you have more?

Yes, I have brought (to help our vows)
Horned poppy, cypress boughs,
The fig-tree wild, that grows on tombs,
And juice that from the larch-tree comes
The basilisk's blood and the viper's skin.
And now our orgies let's begin ...

Jonson wrote some 30 masques to entertain the nobility and none were staged for a paying audience. Usually they would be presented to welcome a distinguished guest to a stately home; as part of the elaborate arrangements for a wedding or a birthday; or to entertain the court during the festive season with courtiers playing the leading roles.

APPENDIX IV

Recommended Reading List

Those taking part in compiling the *Malleus Satani* were asked to give their personal recommendations for a further reading list of books available from libraries and leading book stores. The majority have been written by practising Witches and provide a valuable and factual insight into Craft ritual and belief.

A BOOK OF PAGAN RITUALS: Herman Slater (Weiser 1978 in reprint)
THE DEVIL WITHIN: Marc Cramer (W H Allen 1980)
ELEMENTS OF THE GODDESS: Caitlin Matthews (Element Books 1989)
FIRST STEPS IN RITUAL: Dorlores Ashcroft-Nowicki
                              (Aquarian Press, revised 1990)
LID OFF THE CAULDRON: Patricia Crowther (3rd reprint Weiser NY)
MAGIC IN THE MIDDLE AGES: Richard Kieckhefer (CUP 1990)
THE MEANING OF WITCHCRAFT: Gerald Gardner
                              (Magickal Child 1988 reprint)
NATURAL MAGIC: Doreen Valiente (Hale 1975 - available in reprint)
THE PATH THROUGH THE LABYRINTH: Marion Green
                              (Element Books 1988)
THE PRACTICE OF WITCHCRAFT TODAY: Robin Skelton (Hale 1988)
THE SECRET LIFE OF A SATANIST: Blanche Barton (Mondo USA 1990)
SEX, DISSIDENCE AND DAMNATION: Jeffrey Richards
                              (Routledge 1990)
THE TRUTH ABOUT WITCHCRAFT TODAY: Scott Cunningham
                              (Llewellyn Publications 1988)
VOICES FROM THE CIRCLE: Edited by Prudence Jones & Caitlin
                              Matthews (Aquarian Press 1990)
WICCA - THE OLD RELIGION IN THE NEW AGE: Vivianne Crowley
                              (Aquarian Press 1989)
WITCHCRAFT FOR TOMORROW: Doreen Valiente (Hale 1978)
WITCHCRAFT TODAY: Gerald Gardner (Magickal Child 1988 reprint)
WITCHCRAFT - A TRADITION RENEWED: Evan John Jones (Hale 1990)

Current book lists can be obtained by sending four first class stamps to The Sorcerer's Apprentice, 6/8 Burley Lodge Road, Leeds LS6 1QP

Bibliography & Sources

FRONTIERS OF BELIEF (Marshall Cavendish 1971)
MAN, MYTH & MAGIC, Encyclopedia of the Occult
(Marshall Cavendish 1971)

ANON, The Devil's Prayerbook (Mayflower 1975)
BAIGENT, LEIGH & LINCOLN, The Holy Blood & the Holy Grail
(Cape 1982)
BARTON Blanche, The Secret Life of a Satanist (Mondo USA 1990)**
BEECHSQUIRREL, Nicola, The Pipes of Pan
(Spring 1990; Spring 1989)**
BIRKS & GILBERT, The Treasure of Montsegur (Crucible 1989)
BUCHNER Louis, Force & Matter (Trubner 1864)
CAMMELL C. Aleister Crowley, The Black Magician (NEL 1969)
CATLIN George, North American Indians (Penguin reprint 1989)
CAVE BROWN, Anthony, Bodyguard of Lies (W H Allen 1977)
CAVENDISH Richard, The Magical Arts (Arkana 1984 reprint)
COSTAIN Thomas, The Pageant of England - vols 1 & 2 (Tandem 1973)
CRAMER Marc, The Devil Within (W H Allen 1980)
ELLIOTT Peter, ORCRO Magazine (1990) **
FOLIO, The Witches of Salem (Folio 1982)
FORTUNE Dion, Psychic Self-Defence (Aquarian reprint 1988)
FRAZER Sir James, The Golden Bough (MacMillan 1923 abridged)
FREEDOM Joh, Bad News 1991**
GARDNER Gerald, Witchcraft Today (Jarrolds 1968)
HAINING Peter, The Necromancers (Hodder 1971)
HAMPTON W E, Witchcraft & the Sons of York (Ricardian March 1980)**
HARTMAN Franz, Magic - White & Black (Aquarian 1972 reprint)
HILLS & ROSS, The Great Religions (Crest 1959)
HINNELLS John, A Handbook of Living Religions (Pelican)
HOPE Murry, Practical Celtic Magic (Aquarian 1987)
HOWARD Michael, The Cauldron (Summer issue 1990)**
HOWARD Michael, The Occult Conspiracy (Destiny USA 1989)**
HUSON Paul, Mastering Witchcraft (Berkley 1971)
HUXLEY Aldous, The Devils of Loudun (Folio 1986)
INGLIS Brian, The Paranormal (Paladin 1985)
JAMES Thomas Beaumont, The Palaces of Medieval England
(Sealby 1990)
JOHNS June, King of the Witches (Pan 1969)
JONES & VALIENTE, Witchcraft - A Tradition Renewed (Hale 1990)**

JONSON Ben, Plays & Masques (Norton 1979)
KIECKHEFER Richard, Magic in the Middle Ages (CUP 1990)
KING Francis, Ritual Magic in England (Spearman 1970)
KING & SKINNER, Techniques of High Magic (Sphere 1981 reprint)
LANGER William L, An Encyclopedia of World History (Harrap 1986)
La VEY Anton, The Satanic Bible (Allan 1977)**
LEWIS Matthew, The Monk (Folio reprint 1984)
LOUDAN Jack, The Hell Rakes (Tandem 1967)
McCORMICK Donald, The Hell-Fire Club (Pedigree 1958)
McCORMICK Donald, Murder by Witchcraft (Arrow 1968)
MANNIX Daniel, The Hell-Fire Club (NEL 1970)
MAPLE Eric, The Realm of Ghosts (Robert Hale 1964)
MARLOWE Christopher, Five Plays (Ernest Benn reprint 1960)
MARWICK M. (Ed) Witchcraft & Sorcery (Penguin 1970)
MEADON George Terence, The Goddess of the Stones (Souvenir 1991)
MURRAY Margaret, The God of the Witches (Anchor 1960)
MYERS A. R. England in the Late Middle Ages (Pelican 1986)
PAGAN FEDERATION, The Wiccan (Issues 90 to 96) **
PAULSEN Kathryn, The Complete Book of Magic & Witchcraft
                                          (Signet 1970)
PEARS Cyclopedia (83rd edition)
RICHARDS Jeffrey, Sex, Dissidence & Damnation (Routledge 1992)**
ROBBINS Rossell Hope, The Encyclopedia of Witchcraft & Demonology
                                          (Newnes 1959)
ROBINSON John J. Born in Blood (Guild Publishing 1989)
RUTTER Owen, Scales of Karma (M & J Publishing)
SANDERS Maxine, Maxine, The Witch Queen (Star 1976)
SEZNEC Jean, The Survival of the Pagan Gods (Princetown UP 1953)
SORCERER'S APPRENTICE, The Lamp of Thoth magazine (1988) **
SORCERER'S APPRENTICE, The Occult Census (1989) **
SPRENGER & KRAMER, Malleus Maleficarum (Folio edition 1968)
SYMONDS John, The Great Beast (Mayflower 1973 reprint)
TINDALL Gillian, A Handbook on Witches (Panther 1965)
TONDRIAU & VILLENEUVE, A Dictionary of Devils & Demons
                                          (Gerard 1968)
WAITE Arthur Edward, The Book of Black Magic & Pacts
WILSON Colin, Aleister Crowley - The Nature of the Beast
                                          (Aquarian Press 1987)
WILSON Colin, Mysteries (Granda 1979)
WILSON Colin, The Occult (Mayflower 1973)

ACKNOWLEDGEMENTS:
My grateful thanks must firstly go to Chris Bray and the SAFF without whose invaluable help and advice the work would have been a long and arduous task, if not an impossible one. To Blanche Barton and Anton LaVey of the Church of Satan for their frankness and guidance. Also to Michael Howard for his time and patience; Peter Elliott (and his cat) for access to the ORCRO files; to Paul Greenslade of The Pagan Federation; Meriem Clay-Egerton; Professor Jeffrey Richards; Evan John Jones; Patricia Crowther and John Freedom; to Cole and Rae, Mike, Nicola, Rufus and to all those others who appear in the book for their contribution in giving their views on the broad spectrum of the occult.

** The author would like to thank the publishers and authors for their permission to use quoted material.

INDEX

Ahmed, Rollo:
7, 8, 43-44, 176,
Alexandrians:
17, 27, 86-87, 88,
Anti-Occult Campaign:
15, 16, 17, 20, 28, 87, 93, 115, 158, 162,
Arthur:
49-50,

Baphomet:
67,
Barton, Blanche:
72-74, 156,
Beast, The:
36, 42,
Black Magic (see Magic):
Black Mass, The:
9, 45, 63-67,
Blavatsky, Madame:
29-30,
Book of Revelation:
35-36,
Book of Shadows
(or Witches' Bible):
27,
Bray, Christopher:
17-18, 21, 31, 44, 70-71, 85, 91-92, 96, 104, 109, 117, 124-137, 150-151, 152-155, 176-177,
Bridge of Dreams:
130-131,

Cammell, C. R:
43, 66-67,
Cathars:
10, 52-53, 79, 80, 101,

Cauldron, The:
27, 30,
Celts, The:
41, 49-50, 110,
Cernunnous:
37, 101,
Chambre Ardente Affaire:
64-65,
Church of Satan:
18, 43, 71-77,
Cochrane, Robert:
85, 87, 98-99, 103, 117,
Crowley, Aleister:
19, 42, 43-44, 66-67, 69, 129, 174,
Crowther, Patricia:
28, 86, 99-100, 110-111,
Cursing:
107-108, 170,

Dante (Alighieri):
12, 37-38, 40,
de Guzman, Dominic:
52-53,
de Sade, Marquis:
65-66, 82,
Devil Worship:
8, 9, 10, 25, 33, 43, 51, 70-71, 79, 84, 93, 108, 161,
Divine Comedy, The:
37-38,
Dominican Order, The:
52, 81,
Druids:
49,

Esbats:
51,

Faust:
38-39,
Fertility Cult:
52, 79, 87, 95-96, 97,
Fortune, Dion:
19, 42, 106,
Franciscan Order:
54,
Fundamentalism:
16, 19, 28, 33, 35, 80, 88, 119, 121-123, 128-129, 130-132, 136-137, 140, 152-163, 172,

Gallant, Sandi:
159,
Gardner, Gerald:
20, 21, 27, 85-86, 88, 95-96, 111,
Gardnerians:
17, 86, 88,
Gematria:
36,
God:
29-30, 31, 78, 84-85, 96, 97-98, 101-103, 109,
Goddess:
29-30, 31, 51-52, 78, 81, 96, 97, 101-103, 109-110, 112-113, 117, 148,
Goethe:
38-39,
Golden Bough, The:
52, 95,
Gothic Influences:
12, 40-41,
Grail, The:
42, 49,
Grandier, Urbain:
167,

Great Rite, The:
89-91,
Grimoires:
11, 40, 44, 106, 108,

Halloween (see Samhain):
Hanoverians, The:
62,
Hecate:
51-52,
Hell-Fire Club, The:
12, 65,
Hereditary Witchcraft:
17, 29, 85, 88, 97-99, 103, 112,
Heresy:
10, 11, 53-54, 79-80,
Hermetic Order of the Golden Dawn:
19, 42,
Home Office:
15, 32,
House of Commons:
13, 14, 17, 36, 124-125, 129,
Howard, Michael:
28, 47, 69, 103, 138-139,
Human Zoo, The:
172,
Huysman, J. K:
12, 41,

Initiation:
29, 30, 87, 88-89, 99, 111-112,
Inquisition, The:
10, 11, 19, 52, 54-55, 63, 85, 93, 104,

Jews:
10, 34, 35, 36, 78-79, 101,

Jonson, Ben:
60, 183-5,

Knights Templar:
10, 53, 67, 79, 80, 101,

Lamp of Thoth:
113, 138,
LaVey, Anton:
18, 43, 66, 71-77, 139-140, 156, 171, 173,
Lewis, Mathew:
40-41,
Loudun:
167,

Machen, Arthur:
41-42,
McMartin Pre-School Trial:
13, 158-160,
Magic:
7, 10, 11, 16, 17, 18, 19, 20, 40, 57-58, 104-108, 116-117,
Malleus Malificarum:
10, 20, 44, 81-82,
Marlowe, Christopher:
12, 38,
Masque of Queens:
60, 183-5
Media Coverage:
12-16, 26, 94, 125-128, 134-135, 138-151, 161, 172,
Milton, John:
12, 39-40,
Mori Poll:
150,
Multiple Personality Disorder:
171,

Murray, Dr Margaret:
84-85, 95-96,

New Age:
17, 28, 30, 153-154, 157, 163,
North American Indian Culture:
47-48,

Obscene Kiss, The:
9, 10, 80,
Occult Census, The:
15, 20-32, 68, 69, 77, 126,
Occult Response to the Christian Response to the Occult (ORCRO):
87, 140, 142, 160-161,
Order of the Garter:
56,
Ordo Templis Orientis:
19, 67-68,

Pact:
11,
Pagan Credo, The:
99, 179,
Pagan Federation:
27, 28, 29, 44, 91, 101, 107,
Paganism:
15, 17, 18, 74-75, 79, 85, 98, 102-103, 109-120, 112-113, 138, 173,
Pagan Parenting Network:
113-114,
Pan:
37,
Pipes of Pan, The:
109-110, 112-113,
Plantagenats, The:
55-59,

Possession:
11, 164-169,

Qabalah:
48, 106,

Regardie, Israel:
43,
Reincarnation
26, 99,
Richards, Professor Jeffrey:
10, 11, 78-81, 108,
Robbins, Professor Rossell Hope:
10, 33, 38, 55, 59, 63,
Roman Church:
10, 11, 36, 50-51, 53-54, 56, 57, 78-83, 101, 152, 167,

Sabbat:
9, 63, 84, 89, 98, 100, 104,
St. Anthony's Fire:
169,
Salem:
165-166,
Samhain (Halloween):
100, 141, 157,
Sanders, Alex:
21, 86-87,
Satan
33-46, 73-74, 155,
Satanic Bible:
71, 74, 77,
Satanic Child-Abuse:
13, 14, 20, 26, 27, 63, 93, 95, 113, 115-116, 125, 128, 140-146, 155, 158-159, 161-162,

Satanic Hysteria:
13, 15, 16, 140-146, 157-158, 162, 171-172,
Satanic School:
12,
Satanic Survivors:
9, 12, 15, 16, 20, 44-45, 87-88, 92-93, 140, 171,
Satanism:
7, 9, 13, 16, 17, 25, 26, 63-77, 78, 124, 129, 155, 164, 171, 173,
Sex Magic:
67, 90-92, 173-174,
Shakespeare, William:
59-60,
Shamanism:
47, 95, 96, 110,
Sorcerer's Apprentice, The:
13, 15, 17, 20, 21, 32, 68, 120-121, 124-137, 159,
Stigmata Diaboli
(Devil's mark):
61,
Stonehenge:
48-49,
Stuarts, The:
59-60,
Sub-cultural Alternatives Freedom Foundsation (S.A.F.F.):
31, 32, 44, 129-133, 146-147, 151, 155, 159-160, 162-163, 176, 179,
Summers, Montague:
43-44,

Tudors, The:
59,

Waldensians:
10, 79, 101,
Warboys, Witches of:
167-168,
Wheatley, Denis:
7, 26, 40, 43-44,
White Magic (see Magic):
Wicca:
17, 28, 29, 74-75, 86-87, 88, 92, 95, 103, 112, 115, 149, 155,
Witchcraft:
10, 11, 12, 16, 17, 18, 20, 27, 28, 31, 47-51, 55, 57, 78-80, 82-84, 95-97, 104-105, 107-108, 109-123, 138, 155, 164, 172,
Witchcraft Act:
14, 50, 62, 96,
Witch-Finders:
60-61, 83, 138,
Witch-Trials:
7, 54-55, 61-62, 82, 101,